EAT, DRINK AND
BE MERRY IN MARYLAND

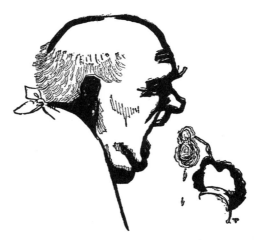

De gustibus non est disputandum

Maryland Paperback Bookshelf

Publisher's Note

Works published as part of the Maryland Paperback Bookshelf are books that are classics of a kind. While some social attitudes have changed and knowledge of our surroundings has increased, we believe that the value of these books as literature, as history, and as timeless perspectives on our region remains undiminished.

Also of Interest in the Series

The Amiable Baltimoreans, by Francis F. Beirne

The Lord's Oysters, by Gilbert Byron

Happy Days: 1880–1892, by H. L. Mencken

Baltimore: When She Was What She Used to Be, 1850–1930,
    by Marion E. Warren and Mame Warren

EAT, DRINK &
BE MERRY IN
MARYLAND

Compiled by
FREDERICK · PHILIP · STIEFF
Illustrated by Edwin Tunis
With a new foreword by Rob Kasper

THE JOHNS HOPKINS UNIVERSITY PRESS
BALTIMORE AND LONDON

Copyright © 1932, 1960, Frederick Philip Stieff
Johns Hopkins Paperbacks edition © 1998 The Johns Hopkins University Press
All rights reserved
Printed in the United States of America on acid-free paper

Johns Hopkins Paperbacks edition, 1998
9 8 7 6 5 4 3 2 1

Illustrations on pp. 33, 83, 93, 97, and 255 copyright © 1957 by Edwin Tunis.
First appeared in *Colonial Living*, published by Thomas Y. Crowell Company.
Reprinted by permission of Curtis Brown, Ltd. Illustrations on pp. 52 and 95 are
courtesy of the Baltimore Museum of Art : gift of Edwin Tunis.

The Johns Hopkins University Press
2715 North Charles Street
Baltimore, Maryland 21218-4319
The Johns Hopkins Press Ltd., London

Library of Congress Cataloging-in-Publication Data

Stieff, Frederick Philip.
    Eat, drink & be merry in Maryland / compiled by Frederick Philip
Stieff ; illustrated by Edwin Tunis : with a new foreword by Rob Kasper.
        p.   cm. — (Maryland paperback bookshelf)
    Reprint. Originally published : New York : G.P. Putnam's Sons, 1932.
    Includes index.
    ISBN 0-8018-5736-8 (alk. paper)
    1. Cookery, American. 2. Cookery—Maryland. I. Title. II. Series.
TX715.S856   1998
641.59752—dc21   97-29895
                                                              CIP
A catalog record for this book is available from the British Library.

TO
OLIVER WENDELL HOLMES

"Baltimore...the gastronomic metropolis of the Union. Why don't you put a canvas-back duck on top of the Washington column? Why don't you get that lady off from the Battle Monument and plant a terrapin in her place? Why will you ask for other glories when you have soft crabs? ...if you open your mouths to speak nature stops them with a fat oyster or offers a slice of the breast of your divine bird."...

OLIVER WENDELL HOLMES
"THE PROFESSOR AT THE BREAKFAST TABLE." 1859

CONTENTS

FOREWORD

T HE terrapin had been bubbling for hours when two cooks paused to consider whether the meat was done. They pulled out a copy of *Eat, Drink, & Be Merry in Maryland.* The well-worn pages informed them that a terrapin should be cooked until its hind legs could be pulled off. This scene, played out some twenty years ago in the Baltimore kitchen of a friend, was my introduction both to terrapin and to Frederick Philip Stieff's 1932 collection of Maryland recipes and culinary lore.

It is a scene unlikely to replayed in many modern kitchens. Now there is a scarcity both of the creatures and of cooks who want to wrestle with them. Thankfully, the charms of this book, reissued now by the Johns Hopkins University Press, extend beyond advice to terrapin boilers. One is that this book not only conveys a sense of place; it celebrates it. In flowing phrases, Stieff describes not merely the aromas and flavors of Maryland fare but also the customs, habits, and homes of the Marylanders who enjoyed it. The blue crab, the prized morsel of the Chesapeake Bay, is extolled as "wholly delicious in hard or in soft states." When the crustacean is served steamed, it must, Stieff advises, be accompanied by beer that is "cold and foamy." A clue to determining a family's social status, Stieff says, is to examine their dining room. "I have yet to see an unimportant dining room in an important Maryland manor."

Stieff, who died in 1964, was an executive in the family business, Charles M. Stieff Piano Co., in Baltimore. When the depression hit in the 1930s, Stieff took advantage of the doldrums in piano sales to pursue his interest in cuisine. Meandering through Maryland, he collected recipes from hotel restaurants, steamships, railroad dining cars, and homesteads. In a newspaper interview published after Stieff's death, members of his family recalled that he had prized any recipe that came to him with pinholes. Old-time Maryland cooks customarily pinned recipes to their shirts, enabling them to lift up and read the instructions as they stood over the stove. For Stieff, a recipe punctured with pinholes was a sign that he had found a winner.

Stieff continued writing about food after his book was published. He wrote a column chronicling his dining adventures for *Gardens, Houses, and People,* a monthly journal aimed at Baltimore's upper crust. (He wrote about other topics as well. Active in civic affairs, he penned a series of articles for the *Sun* in the 1950s, describing how Los Angeles, Chicago, and other growing cities were taking steps to cope with traffic congestion.)

While the book's tie to the past is its strong point, that link also contributes to its weakness. The patrician tone, found both in Stieff's writing and in the illustrations by Edwin Tunis, can be jarring. Ladies are lovely examples of "vivacious femininity." Servants, housewives, and farmers are characterized as not too bright and are the object of many jokes. In reissuing this sixty-five-year-old work, the Johns Hopkins Press eliminated the illustrations it considered racist. The past is not always pretty.

Unlike today's recipes, which are written for a populace that regards cooking as a novel undertaking, the recipes in Stieff's book address veterans of the kitchen. The reader is simply told to split a partridge; no further instructions are assumed to be needed. Measurements tend to be given either in gargantuan proportions, a mincemeat pie recipe, for example, yields fifteen pies; or in quaint terms, such as the direction to use a lump of butter the size of an egg. Baking is done in either a "quick oven" or a "slack oven," with no mention of Fahrenheit or centigrade.

I found surprises in the recipes. There is okra, a staple of the South, in the crab soup served at Baltimore's old Rennert Hotel. There is much more pepper than I expected, cayenne in the Emerson Hotel's Crab Flake Maryland, liberal amounts of black pepper on the soft crabs made by Mrs. R. E. Bradley of Baltimore, and cayenne again in the macaroni made by Miss Rebecca French of Washington County. The old folks led spicier lives than I had imagined, an insight that could probably apply to a variety of topics and a variety of generations.

A few Maryland-born "celebrities," such as etiquette expert Emily Post and author Christopher Morely, contributed recipes to the book. But the real luminaries seem to be the grand estates of Maryland, such as Sotterly in St. Mary's County, and Hampton in Baltimore County. Their architecture is extolled and recipes from their kitchens are related in worshipful prose.

It is hard to predict how an old book will be assessed by modern readers. Historians might appreciate this book's strong sense of regional pride and the importance it gives to details of domestic life. Ambitious cooks might be inspired to recreate dishes from a time when homegrown ingredients—oysters from the Patuxent River, cantaloupe from the fields of the Eastern Sho', stuffed hams from St. Mary's county—were the norm.

Eat, Drink & Be Merry in Maryland made this modern day trenchermen feel a twinge of jealousy. Reading accounts of the days when folks dined on fish pulled from the Chesapeake instead of from a freezer, and when bread came from the hot oven instead of a crowded grocery store, I was sorry I had missed so many good meals. Stieff's words made me want to follow the ways of those who discovered the joy of spending an evening with a planked rockfish and garniture of vegetables, of folks who knew that a key to living well in Maryland is enjoying your time at its table.

—ROB KASPER

A LETTER FROM EMILY POST

MY DEAR MR. STIEFF,

The sentiment of a word! I know now that had you labeled the proofs you sent me "Recipes" I should have thought "Another cook book!" and gone no further with it. But your collection of Old Maryland Receipts awakens a thousand memories; brings a nostalgia for my native State, and for a beautiful hospitality that was not expressed by a dinner on the tenth, nor a lunch party on the fourteenth, but by an unceasing gathering of visitors as well as kin around its tables of abundance on every day the whole year through.

A daily dinner party at three o'clock mid-afternoon (what an hour!). A lavish high tea—wasn't it at nine o'clock? My memory seems limited to a single picture of many candles mirrored in the polished mahogany surface of a vast table, and of a black band of wrist between the white cotton glove and pulled-up coat-sleeve of Old James, the butler, as he reached over and lifted the huge domed silver cover off of a platter piled high with fried oysters. It may have been part of the same picture, or of another one, in which the light of a bright log fire danced on the carved tops of the Chippendale chairs, at about eye-level, as I walked by to the end of the table adorned with that gleaming beauty, a Kirk tea service ornamented with castles and trees, and from which I received a sip of chocolate with a taste of whipped cream on it; before saying "Good-night."

More vividly still, as I write this to you, comes the memory of the early morning sound of beating biscuits; the thump thump of the end of a flat-iron beating into the biscuit dough, accenting Louisa's unceasing hymn-singing—on and on seemingly for hours! When the beating stopped it was time to rush through dressing and down to breakfast. Memory of breakfast is a jumble of peaches, cream with lumps of richness in it, grits, kidney-stew, herring-roe, coddled eggs, sausages, griddle cakes, milk so rich it left a thick white "French mustache" unless one was very careful not to dip one's lips too deep.

Other memories are of chickens plucked to an accompaniment of Negro harmony; terrapin in the cellar shutting themselves into their houses tight and then suddenly nipping the toes of a yelping dog named Toby; partridges and canvas-backs "hanging" upon a kitchen wall. Nor can any Marylander hear the word Madeira without the vision of Georgian dining rooms, and that after-dinner ritual when the cloth was removed and cigars, dishes of nuts and raisins, and decanters in their coasters, were put on. Sometimes the ladies and children lingered, sometimes they withdrew, but the gentlemen smoked, nibbled nuts, sipped their wine and talked over—the morning's editorials in the "Sun-paper."

All of which is a long way to say that it seems to me that the title of your book tells the whole story. "Drinking in Maryland" awakens memories not only of the old gentlemen's fairly frequent mint-juleps, the old ladies' occasional milk punches, flavored with sherry-wine! the potent eggnog of New Year's day, and the after-dinner glass of Madeira—all of which, though truly "drinking," was limited, it must be remembered, by the sobriety which Society exacted of its gentlemen. Eating in Maryland was a continuous feast, not alone because of the prodigality of its table, but because of the warmth of its ever welcoming hospitality. And certainly it seems to me that in this book of yours the traditions of Maryland's hospitality, no less than those merely of its kitchens, will be preserved for all time.

With all best wishes for a great success,

Very sincerely yours,

New York.

PREFACE

I take as my text this morning the eighth chapter of Ecclesiastes, the fifteenth verse: "Then I commended mirth, because a man hath no better thing under the sun, than to eat, and to drink, and to be merry." That there may be other sentiments contained within the covers of the Holy Writ which more aptly conform to the Marylander's aspect of life is possible, I admit, but highly improbable. And here, I might add, endeth the reading of the first lesson. From the research which I have enjoyed, it seems to me that ever since those destined to become the original Marylanders landed in St. Mary's County in the *Ark* and the *Dove* in 1634, Marylanders have established for themselves an unassailable reputation as builders de luxe of dining rooms. It is quite evident that the conception, location, and furnishing of the dining room were the culmination, the climax, of their anticipation of accomplishing a purpose—that of eating, of drinking, and of being merry.

While I do not wish to imply that the original Marylanders were alone in the good fortune of their origin, the fact remains that the early settlers of our fair state were from the finest flower of Old England's gentry. They were in most instances thoroughly proficient in the higher art of living—or the art of high living, as you may wish. They had stamina, plenty of it, they were well acquainted with good sports, fine horse flesh, a pretty face, a dainty ankle, an abundant cuisine, a well stocked cellar, and the gout. Naturally the dining rooms had to be well designed to accommodate and grace hunt breakfasts, a vivacious femininity, in close proximity to an equally well designed and well equipped kitchen, and not too far from the cellar.

In all my Maryland meanderings, I have yet to see an unimportant dining room in an important Maryland manor. On the contrary, practically every such dining room has more background—if the manor be of sufficiently early vintage—than all the rest of the house. Before leaving this hallowed sanctuary we might comment in passing on the elastic capacity of the great table, on the knife and fork urns or boxes upon the sideboard, the cellarette beneath it, the museum-like display of glassware within the corner cupboard with its sparkling ruby, amethyst, emerald, and ultramarine scintillation. The carved cornices and pillars—probably completed by an indentured slave—are well worthy of comment, the wall paneling, the lavish display of silver and pewter upon the sideboard, as well as the "black-jack" * thereon as at Montpelier, and the toddy table near by as in the Hammond-Harwood House at Annapolis, all contribute in mute eloquence toward the natural determination of the Marylander "to eat, to drink, and to be merry."

And quite frequently, when the windows of these culinary shrines are opened high, it is possible to part the low doors beneath that the guests may pass through and down the steps into the box-burdened garden, pungent and heavy in the night air of spring with the perfume of lilac, wistaria, "valley" and magnolia.

* A leathern tankard used for ale and beer.

From the garden we well observe the pantries with their restless activity of colored servants "fetching and toting," and the spacious kitchen beyond. And what a kitchen! Highly technical in its equipment, it resembles equally the den of an alchemist as it does Aunt 'Liza's laboratory. Quite frequently back of this culinary shrine lie the slave quarters, as in the Roger Brooke Taney House in Frederick. And not a great distance away the "smokehouse" where those tribal ceremonies so frequently took place about a hickory wood fire on "sunshiny days," to the ultimate glory and memorialization of Maryland hams.

There can scarcely be any question but that Maryland cellars have perhaps more old-world "atmosphere" than any other portion of a Marylander's castle. A descent into some of these dungeons adequately subtantiates such an assertion. In fact there are cellars, such as that of the Hammond-Harwood House, which seem to me to resemble more the dungeons of the Castel Sant' Angelo than do the dungeons of Sant' Angelo themselves. The remarkable thickness of the walls and partitions, the graceful arches which must have formed concentric segments above the casks once beneath them, instill within one the desire to follow the contents of those casks back up again into the candle-lit dining room above.

Quite possibly might we find a Madeira party in full progress—six to twenty or more decanters of amber liquid upon the table with a goodly number of glasses at each place. Regardless of the normal habits of the guests, on such occasions as this tobacco was taboo, that the atmosphere might be clear from the noxious fumes to permit the contestants the better to discern the minutiæ of differentiation between the contents of the decanters. For these were contests to the death, the death possibly of a gentleman's reputation as a connoisseur of the finer wines of life. And the conversation—what strange language it seems to us moderns:—under what circumstances wines could be bruised, what foods were most complementary with what wines and what vintages, and on what occasions; what wines and vintages improve with age and for what period does this improvement continue until some, like the human mind, break under their own burden and lose "body"; what temperature is ideal for the indulgence of Madeira, of Sherry or of Port, and how long each should remain in the room in which it is to be consumed prior thereto. Small differences, you say? Yet how easy for small differences to transform a gentleman of the Old School into an old gentleman who needs schooling.

But not for a brief moment must it be supposed that connoisseurship—if I may be permitted the term—was confined to those of bibulous intent. On the contrary, the ladies were apparently quite avariciously inclined when it came to augmenting their already astounding compendium of culinary information. Indeed, it would be difficult, if possible at all, to discover a family receipt book the pages of which were not interspersed with receipts in many handwritings garnered from many sources. Whereas in our youth many of us philatelically inclined would have thrilled at the opportunity of trading a triangular "Cape of Good Hope" for an early issue of "Mauritius" it is quite evident that our feminine progenitors experienced a similar thrill in exchanging a "mushroom soup" for a "plum pudding." Nor were the receipts sought after confined to those dishes strictly indigenous to the Free State. To suppose so is to err sadly. Marylanders loved to live and enjoyed a receipt if good, from a foreign clime, equally as they did one the origin of which might have been strictly local. If the concoction were worthy of the kitchen and dining room, the family and guests, it was indeed a worthy addition to the culinary experience of the hostess. It is just as true today. I have "spaghettied" from Ventimiglia to Brindisi and I doubt if I have ever eaten as excellent spaghetti, certainly none better nor richer, than I have enjoyed in the home of a very charming Maryland hostess. A glance at the menu of the famous railway dinner of 1857, three-quarters of a century ago—a copy of which you may find in the appendix—is sufficient testimony that Marylanders did indulge beyond oysters, spoon bread, ham and fried chicken.

Similarly is the evidence afforded by the bills for entertaining, copies of which are also included in the appendix. Of course Marylanders have never been able to celebrate or entertain efficiently without eating, drinking and being quite merry. Consequently it is not surprising to find items on these historical documents such as "98 bottles of wine, 2½ gal. spirits, 'musick,' attendance in the bar 35, 12 packs of cards"—these items from an "Account for an Entertainment to His Excelly. Gen. Washington the 22nd Dec. 1783" at Annapolis and charged to the State. And again on the 4th of Dec. 1784 the worthy General was entertained by the State, and on this bill we find "42 bottles Madeira, 21 bottles of port wine, four gallons spirits, 4 [packs] cards, 'musick,' attendance at the bar 15." And when they celebrated in April 1783, again at the expense of the State, the news of peace with England, forsooth, they gave their thanks in lusty fashion. For example, upon the bill we find 116 gallons wine and six gallons spirits, and the gargantuan quantities of red meats would certainly indicate a huge or hungry crowd, or both. They had a ball on this occasion though they apparently did not confine themselves to terpsichorean delights for we find charges upon the bill for [packs] cards, 24, eight more gallons of wine and four of spirits.

It is interesting to reduce the wines and spirits consumed on these three state occasions to quarts—a "bottle of wine" as billed, to be one quart, and a gallon of spirits to be four quarts. Thus we have 657 quarts of wine and 66 quarts of spirits, a ratio of practically ten to one in favor of the lighter intoxicant. From this one may deduce as one pleases.

The disciples of the modern school of dietetics will probably object to the terms of measurement "the size of an egg," "the size of a walnut," "a pinch," "a handful" or "a dot of butter," salt and pepper "according to taste," although the terms "a teaspoonful," "a tablespoonful," "a teacupful" are somewhat more exact. It must not be overlooked that much of Maryland culinary supremacy is due to the kitchen skill of the early slaves and their descendants. In many instances 'Liza and her contemporaries did not know how to read or write much less how to juggle drams and pennyweights or to know just how hot her oven had to be to register 236 degrees Fahrenheit. It still remains true that the proof of not only the pudding, but of everything that is cooked, is in the eating. For several centuries Maryland's reputation for cooking seems to have survived, and judging from the frequent references to Baltimore, Chesapeake, and Maryland on menus in this country and abroad there still appears to be quite a definite demand for it. Let me suggest to those conscientious objectors to the more informal school of measurement that they invest in an egg and a walnut and keep these upon the kitchen shelf for standard measurement and that they reduce the "pinches," "handfuls," "dots," etc., to their exact Troy equivalents—"to suit their taste."

Similarly I have made practically no changes in the language used. Granted that it would prove no insurmountable task to transform this language into eighth grade English, I have preferred to copy from manuscript, feeling that much of the charm would be lost by editing or paraphrasing. Marylanders are still using, with very few exceptions, the receipts as quoted in this collection and I certainly do not attribute less ingenuity of interpretation to those outside our boundaries.

In fact, it has always been difficult to persuade an old-time darky to give her receipts in language that could be followed and in many instances where these receipts have been accompanied by such note as "Betsy's receipt" or "by Becky Perkins" they have been recorded only through the collaboration of the mistress of the manor.

No receipts in this volume have been taken from a printed page. Each one has been obtained at the source, either sent in by the contributor upon request or, as in many instances, copied from age-stained family receipt books of every vintage up to and over one hundred years old. Some few have been included for "atmosphere" such as those for isinglass jelly but with these few exceptions endeavor has been made that all are practical of adoption by any modern couple just starting their culinary experiences.

A separate chapter on "The Cooking and Stuffing of Hams and the Curing of Meats after the Fashion of old Maryland Manors" was included advisedly. The curing of meats, particularly hams, has been an old and revered Maryland custom. The "smoke-house" was as much an integral part of the ménage of a Maryland manor as the slave quarters or the stables. And the cult of curing and aging was confined not to the gentler sex but more often supervised by the lord of the manor himself. Similarly the process of stuffing these hams was a pride of the entire family. Easter is the time elected for neighborhood competition and hospitality. Open house is still held in rural districts at Easter and progressive groups make the rounds to sample the culinary craftsmanship in the art of stuffing hams. I believe the conclusions are invariably identical—all are conceded to be excellent, but not up to the standard of the visitors' own system. I am inclined to agree with each beyond question.

The cuisine of Maryland is surely the most diversified of any similar area in the country. Consultation with our gastronomic map is ample assurance. Far be it from me to compare degrees of excellence. It is of course only natural that those counties bordering on the Bay should specialize in "Sea Food" and migratory waterfowl. In Western Maryland big game and game fish prevail and we find more frequently receipts calling for buckwheat and maple syrup which are pridefully indigenous to this section. There is in these western counties an influence of German or Pennsylvania Dutch in the cooking since they lie just across the Mason-Dixon line from the rural districts of Pennsylvania.

There is much to be learned from these old family receipt

books. I have perused many of earlier date than a century ago. While I have known that Bombay Duck is not duck nor even fowl, but fish, and realized that there are no plums in plum pudding, no nuts in doughnuts and should be no sand in sand tarts, I must confess that it was a revelation never to find one mention of cheese outside of the title in the receipts of that old favorite dish "cheese cake." It has been a temptation to include many of these receipts invariably found recurring in these family annals yet none of which, fortunately, ever find themselves upon the dining-room table. I refer to such instructions as: to take grease from clothes, to make ink, varnish for boots and shoes, cures for croup, neuralgia, dropsy, a pleasant spring medicine, worm mixture, cough drops, cologne, to destroy rats and mice, silver polish, Gen. Twigg's Hair Dye, how to dye a royal purple, to restore a black color when faded. Space prohibits their inclusion in this volume but they are none the less interesting. In the days when such family remedies were collected it must not be lost sight of that the family doctor did not live around the corner, could not be reached by phone nor arrive by motor. Nor was it possible to obtain the services of a cleaning and dyeing establishment on the way to the office or to market in the morning.

In fact, there can be no vague hope to do the cuisine of Maryland justice in a single volume. If justice is desired then several book shelves, each exceeding the famous dimensions of that of Dr. Eliot's, must be filled. The most that can be hoped for in a single volume is a generalization, a diversification of the receipts which have for decades of a century and more contributed toward the gastronomic supremacy of Maryland. The five hundred and more receipts which compose this volume have been culled from twice that number on hand, over a hundred sources, from every county in the State, and including those originating on the manor, from the towns and cities, the inns, hotels, clubs,—town, country and sporting—and from rail and boat. As previously stated, in no instance has any been taken from a printed page. All have been obtained without exception at the source.

And not alone has culinary knowledge made this volume possible. Too much credit cannot be given to those whose names appear in his book for their courtesy, coöperation and interest and for the assistance which they have so unstintingly rendered, and their willingness to delve deep into family annals that the world may share the secrets of the cult of Maryland cooking. That this humble effort of compilation may seem to justify to some small degree their coöperation is as much as the compiler dare hope.

And to Emily Post and Mayor Howard Jackson of Baltimore, I am deeply indebted and appreciative for their words of encouragement not only as herein expressed but as given from time to time during the process of compilation. Similarly do I value the assistance of Miss Elisabeth Amery, Supervisor of Home Economics of the State Department of Education, whose counsel has been invaluable in the mechanics of classifications and who has given so freely of her time and experience.

I sincerely trust that this collection of receipts so limited by space may give pleasure to those still interested in the fine art of living and that it may assist the stranger within our gates "to Eat, to Drink" and ever "to Be Merry in Maryland."

—FREDERICK PHILIP STIEFF

SOUPS

CHICKEN GUMBO SOUP

Cut and wash one large chicken, put it in five quarts of water, add one large can tomatoes, one half a chopped onion, some celery. Boil until chicken is tender. Remove chicken and strain soup, adding one pint okra, several diced potatoes, one cup rice, three ears corn, one cup lima beans. Return to fire and boil until vegetables are done. Cut chicken from bone and return to soup, seasoning highly with salt and pepper.—*Mrs. Bernard Freeman, Baltimore.*

BLACK BEAN SOUP

Soak overnight in cold water 1 pint beans. Put the beans in 6 quarts cold water with ½ lb. salt pork, a beef bone, 1 onion, 1 carrot, 1 turnip, one teaspoonful cloves. Boil three or four hours. Then strain through colander, add a little cornstarch, thicken and boil a few minutes longer. Serve with slices of lemon and hard boiled egg.—*Mrs. Charles B. Trail, Frederick County.*

CHICKEN SAGO SOUP

1 quart of water in which a chicken has been boiled, 3 tablespoonfuls of the best pearl sago soaked in cup of cold water, 1 cup of cream heated to boiling, the yolks of 2 eggs, beaten light. Warm the soaked sago by putting the cup in a pan of hot water, stirring from time to time. Then stir it in the broth, simmer for an hour taking care that it does not burn, beat in the cream and eggs, give one good boil-up and serve.—*The Misses Reynolds, Rose Hill Manor Inn, Frederick County.*

CLAM CHOWDER

(6 persons)

Pint of fish broth, pint of clam liquor brought to a boil, add one sliced onion, two diced potatoes, small amount of diced salt pork and boil until barely done, then add one and a half dozen scalded clams, diced. Season with salt, pepper and mace and bring to boil again.—*Hotel Rennert, Baltimore.*

CELERY SOUP

Boil celery until soft, then press through a sieve. To one pint of stock, made of veal or chicken, add the celery. To thicken it, take a tablespoonful of butter and two tablespoonfuls of flour, season with pepper and salt, and strain so it will be perfectly smooth. Put it back on fire in a double boiler. A cupful of cream is then added.—*Mrs. J. Alexis Shriver, Olney, Harford County.*

CLAM CHOWDER

Open and mince fifteen clams. Peel and cut fine four or five medium round potatoes and one large onion, cut in discs. Fry two slices of bacon cut in small pieces, a stalk of celery cut fine, two medium tomatoes. Put all together and cook until potatoes are nearly soft. Then add the clams and liquor and boil for ten minutes or more. Mix one teaspoonful flour with a little water and add to the mixture and cook for two minutes longer.—*Mrs. J. B. Tawes, Somerset County.*

OLNEY

(*"Olney," Harford County, the home of Mr. and Mrs. J. Alexis Shriver, is one of the most fascinating in this section of the State. The home, started in 1810, was sold to the father of the present owner in 1861. Ever since, its beauty has been added to by the owners and the grounds have become a fairyland of box, magnolias, crepe myrtle, yew and bamboo. Among the most interesting features of the home are the majestic Ionic columns that were once a part of the Athenæum Club of Baltimore, and the marble medallion over the door of the portico, which medallion was originally designed by L'Enfant, who laid out the City of Washington.*)

BLACK BEAN SOUP

1 quart black beans, a knuckle of raw veal, 2 onions, 2/3 tumbler wine (Sherry is best), 1 lemon, 3 or 4 eggs, ½ tablespoonful of cloves, ½ tablespoonrul of allspice, pepper, salt. Soak the beans overnight. In the morning turn off the water, and

add 7 quarts of fresh water and the raw veal. Let this boil one hour, skim well, add onions, cut fine, cloves, allspice, pepper and salt. Boil 3 hours longer. Strain through a colander, rubbing the beans gently. Cut some of the meat in ½ inch pieces. Add them to the soup. Put the meat back in the pot, and the wine and the lemon sliced and quartered. Let it boil up three or four times. Have ready in the tureen the eggs boiled hard and sliced, and forcemeat balls, made quite small. Pour the soup on them, leaving out the knuckle of veal (1877).—*Mr. J. Alexis Shriver, Olney, Harford County.*

SOUP À LA BISQUE

One and one-half pints of milk, one can of tomatoes. Boil and strain the tomatoes, add a pinch of baking soda, a lump of butter the size of an egg, a little pepper and salt. Thicken with a tablespoonful of corn starch dissolved in a little cold milk. Put the milk to boil separately and add just before serving.—*Miss Eliza Thomas, Baltimore.*

CRAB GUMBO SOUP

To a small knuckle of veal put a quarter of a peck of okra cut up, a dozen and a half large tomatoes, one onion, three long red peppers, one of them chopped up and the other two whole, parsley.—Let it boil 6 hours. About one hour before dinner put in 6 boiled hard crabs, a little broken up, shells and all, but not picked. A small piece of bacon improves it. Press through colander removing knuckle and shells.—*Mrs. Charles H. Tilghman, Gross' Coate, Talbot County.*

GROSS' COATE

("GROSS' COATE" *cannot but interest any one who appreciates the atmosphere of a dignified English home. Situated overlooking the beautiful Wye River it requires but little to imagine oneself on the banks of the Thames, excepting that there is not the turbulent river life of the latter although in the humble opinion of the writer far more beauty. Granted to Roger Gross in 1660 Gross' Coate came into the possession of the Tilghman family in 1748 in whose possession it has remained ever since. The gardens, laid out with utmost discrimination, lead down to the private pier and landing, and complete another picture of a perfect Maryland Manor.*)

WHITE CRAB SOUP

Steam six crabs, crack the legs and fins and put them in a gallon of water with the fat from the backs. Season to taste. While the above is boiling about one and a half hours, pick the crabs and after draining off the water from legs and fins put liquid back in pot with prepared crabs and let boil one-half hour. Pour one-half pint of cream in tureen and serve.

Seasoning:—A slice of fresh middling, pepper and if you like it a little onion, and one quarter pound of butter rubbed into a tablespoonful of flour.—*Mrs. T. Rowland Thomas, Baltimore.*

7

CORN SOUP

One can corn, one pint cold water, one quart heated milk, two teaspoons butter, one teaspoon chopped onion, two teaspoons flour, two teaspoons salt, one-quarter teaspoon white pepper, yolks of two eggs. Cook the corn 20 minutes. Melt the butter, add the chopped onion, and cook until light brown; add the flour and when thoroughly mixed, add the milk gradually. Add this mixture to the corn and season with salt and pepper. Rub through a sieve. Then heat again. Beat the yolks of the eggs, put them into a soup tureen, and pour the soup over them slowly. Serve as soon as mixed. Thicken soup with cornstarch and butter. This prevents the separation of the thicker and thinner parts of the soup.—*Mrs. J. Alexis Shriver, Olney, Harford County.*

CRAB GUMBO SOUP

Put one can of tomatoes into four quarts of water, add a few blades of mace, three stalks of celery cut in small pieces. Boil until the tomatoes are done, then strain, return to fire adding one cup of rice, two white potatoes cut in small pieces, one half cup of corn, one pint of okra cut in small pieces. Cook until vegetables are tender, then add one pint of crab flakes. Season highly with pepper and salt to taste.—*Mrs. Bernard Freeman, Baltimore.*

CONSOMMÉ

Take four pounds of rump of beef, salt it and put on the fire with three quarts of cold water, one peeled Irish potato, two carrots, one turnip, one onion, the top of a bunch of celery, three bay leaves, pepper and salt to taste, parsley and a little tomato.

Let all boil slowly for six or seven hours, adding more water when it boils down to keep it to three quarts. Then take off the fire, strain off vegetables. Let the liquor stand all night well covered. In the morning remove every particle of grease. Put the stock on the fire, let it heat thoroughly, stirring in white of an egg and shells to clear it. Strain and add a glass of sherry wine and a tablespoonful of caromel made of brown sugar burnt and stirred with water until it is a thick liquor. For Julienne soup add vegetables cut in small pieces.—*Dr. Walter Forman Wickes, Wickcliffe, Greenspring Valley, Baltimore County.*

MUSHROOM SOUP

Boil half a pound of mushrooms until tender, then mash through a sieve. Put the mushrooms back into the water in which they were boiled. When they come to a boil add one quart of rich milk, two tablespoons of flour, and butter the size of egg.—*Mrs. Charles Wickes Whaland, M.D., Kent County.*

MULLIGATAWNY SOUP

2 old fowls, 1 young fowl, 4 quarts water, cream, curry powder. Stew down two fowls in four quarts water, to half the quantity. Have young fowl cut in small pieces, thicken soup with a little cream, flour and curry powder, and the livers of the fowls parboiled and beaten in a mortar. Then put in pieces of fowl and let all simmer about one hour. Serve with boiled rice.—*Mrs. Robert Goldsborough Henry, Myrtle Grove, Talbot County.*

9

CRAB SOUP SHORE STYLE

(8 persons)

Put two ounces butter, one chopped onion and one chopped green pepper in casserole and simmer until done, add two quarts of fish broth, one-half cup of rice and boil slowly for fifteen minutes. Add three peeled tomatoes diced, one teaspoonful of Worcestershire sauce, the meat of two large crabs, one pound of fresh okra or one can of okra cut in pieces one inch long. Cook slowly twenty minutes, season well with salt and pepper, sprinkle with a little chopped parsley.—*Hotel Rennert, Baltimore.*

MOCK TURTLE SOUP

Sauté carrots, turnips, onions and shallots. Add to them some browned veal and beef bones in good stock. Put in a little vinegar, thyme, bay leaves, cloves and mace. Bring to a boil, skim. Now add calf's head. Boil till done; take up, skin, press and cut into dice. Thicken the stock with roux, strain and add the cubes of calf's head and some chopped hard boiled egg. Add salt, cayenne and lemon juice.—*Mr. H. B. Grimshaw, Baltimore Steam Packet Co., Baltimore.*

TOMATO SOUP

One pint of tomatoes stewed as for the table; add one pint water and boil ten minutes; put in one teaspoonful soda and skim. Add pepper and salt and piece of butter the size of an egg. Thicken with flour or cracker crumbs, add one pint of milk and let it boil.—*Mrs. J. Morsell Roberts, Calvert County.*

DEEP FALLS

MUSHROOM SOUP

One-half pound of mushrooms, one pint of milk, one half pint of cream, salt and pepper to taste, two tablespoonsful flour, two squares of butter.

Cut mushrooms in small pieces and boil in salt water twenty-five minutes. Heat milk and cream, add mushrooms, a little of the essence, add thickening (flour, pepper, salt and butter; melt butter and add flour, pepper and salt to taste). When all boils, add chopped parsley. If only cream is used in place of milk it will be much richer. When serving add a little whipped cream on top of each cupful.—*Mrs. James B. Parran, Deep Falls, St. Mary's County.*

OYSTER SOUP

Strain one quart of oysters in a colander. Put liquor in sauce-pan with two tablespoonsful of chopped celery, one tablespoonful of onion, one half teaspoonful of salt, a little pepper and one sprig of thyme. When boiling, add oysters with one large table-spoonful of butter rubbed into two tablespoonsful of flour. Cook until oysters are well plumped, add one pint of hot milk, let the soup come to a boil and serve at once.—*Mrs. James B. Parran, Deep Falls, St. Mary's County.*

OYSTER SOUP

One quart oysters. Strain oysters through the colander and put liquor to boil with tablespoon chopped celery, one teaspoon finely chopped onion and one sprig of thyme—pepper and salt.

Add oysters and cook until the gills curl. Then add one tablespoon butter creamed with one tablespoon flour. When this boils add one pint of milk. Let all come to a boil and serve at once.—*Mrs. John H. Sothoron, The Plains, St. Mary's County.*

TO MAKE PEPPER POT

Take four pounds of tripe and one knuckle of veal and boil them separately until perfectly tender, then cut them in small pieces and put them in the liquor the veal was boiled in. Add a few force-meat balls, about ten potatoes cut small, a handful of sweet marjoram, a little sweet basil, a few cloves and pepper and salt to taste, then let all boil about two hours.—*Mrs. J. Alexis Shriver, Olney, Harford County.*

VEGETABLE SOUP

Procure good beef bone for soup stock, wash and place in large kettle covered with cold water. Add one cup lima beans, either fresh or dried, one cup Navy beans, one quarter cup of rice, four ears of corn cut from the cob, or one can of shoe-peg corn, three tomatoes cut fine or one small can of tomatoes, one each of turnip, carrot and potato all diced, one onion chopped fine, two sprigs celery cut fine, one tablespoon minced parsley, two large leaves of cabbage shredded, one tablespoonful Worcestershire sauce, one quarter teaspoonful each of ground cloves and nutmeg and a dash of thyme leaves, one small hot red pepper, one can tomato soup. Add salt and pepper to taste. Let come to good boil, then reduce heat and boil slowly for good rich soup.

This makes a good deal, but you know, "Soup is always better the second day."—*Mrs. J. H. Windsor, Windsor Manor, Baltimore County.*

POTATO SOUP

Boil four potatoes, mash them fine, and add one egg, a piece of butter the size of an egg; one-half teaspoonful of salt, a little essence of celery or celery seed. Boil one pint water, one pint of milk, turn it on the potatoes, stir it well and send it to the table hot.—*Mrs. Wm. Courtland Hart, Somerset County.*

OYSTERS

CHRISTOPHER MORLEY

(ONLY *Christopher Morley could be more interesting than the characters he creates. No age has failed to delight in his whimsicalities, his humor and his philosophy. Although one of Maryland's most versatile littérateurs, his pen never forsakes the realm of charm in which he ever maintains that delightful freshness that brings youth and experience to the edge of a literary fountain, which, had it existed in the days of Ponce de Leon, might well have caused that worthy adventurer to cease his search.)*

17

My dear Fred Stieff:

I've been so deplorably hard run—trying to work on a book myself—that I haven't had a chance to dig up any traditional formulæ—and then I'm only a pseudo-Marylander anyhow and have no right to fry chicken in your skillet.

But if you really want a recipe from the heart, it would go like this:—

On a fine spring or autumn day (preferably April or October; months with an R) take one B. & O. bus from any of several convenient Depots in N. Y. City. Mix with this a North River ferryboat to Jersey City and a comfortable uncrowded ride on B. & O. express (4½ hrs. approx.).—Let stand for 2 minutes to cool in Mount Royal Station, the world's most agreeable Railroad halt—

Then take a taxi in whatever direction you please and you will find good food, good drink, and good companions. If I had my free choice I should want a good old Park Avenue oyster stew such as we used to have at home when all the world was young.

Yours,
Christopher Morley.

OYSTER COCKTAILS

For two dozen small oysters, make the following mixture: One tablespoonful of horseradish, half teaspoonful Tabasco sauce, one tablespoonful each of vinegar and Worcestershire sauce, two tablespoonsful of lemon juice, one tablespoonful tomato catsup and half teaspoonful salt. Mix thoroughly and set in the ice box for an hour before serving.—*Col. D. Charles Winebrener, Frederick County.*

OYSTERS, CHESAPEAKE STYLE

Dry oysters on a towel, sauté in butter, sprinkle flour over them, sauté until brown, season with salt and pepper, then cook one slice of bacon, put on top, then put brown gravy around same on platter.—*Dining Car Service, B. & O. R.R.*

OYSTERS IN CHAFING DISH

(3 persons)

Two dozen select oysters, two stalks celery, one quarter pound butter, one-half teaspoon of salt, one-quarter teaspoon black pepper. Cut celery about half inch long, place in chafing dish, cover with water and cook. Place oysters on celery, add butter, salt and pepper, cook until edges of oysters begin to curl —*Hotel Rennert, Baltimore.*

OYSTER FRICASSEE

Two quarts of oysters, thoroughly washed—one cup butter— one cup cream—one tablespoonful of flour mixed in a little milk —the yolks of three eggs, well beaten. Put the butter in a pan and let it come to a boil—add the oysters—let them simply cook, then take off the stove and add cream, flour and a little pepper. Put back upon the stove and let come to a boil—then stir in quickly the yolks of the eggs. Take off the stove at once and serve on a platter of hot buttered toast.—*Mrs. Bartlett S. Johnston, Baltimore.*

FRIED OYSTERS

Wash and drain one pint of large oysters. Salt and pepper to taste. Have ready two plates filled with cracker meal and two well beaten eggs to which have been added two tablespoonsful of milk. Dip oysters first in cracker meal, then beaten egg, then cracker meal again. Fry a few at a time in hot grease, drain on brown paper.—*Mrs. J. B. Tawes, Somerset County.*

CREAMED OYSTERS IN PATTY-SHELLS

Wash oysters and scald slightly. Make a dressing of one cup of milk, butter the size of an egg, one tablespoonful flour and cook until thick. Salt and pepper to taste. A little parsley cut fine will add to them if liked. Add cream to oysters, fill patty-shells and serve hot.—*Mrs. J. B. Tawes, Somerset County.*

BAKED OYSTERS LAFAYETTE

One dozen medium oysters, freshly open on the deep shell, prepare an oyster cocktail sauce adding one chopped shallot and pour over the raw oysters, garnish the top of oysters with a piece of thin bacon cut the same length as oyster shell, sprinkle with bread crumbs, add small piece of butter on each oyster and bake in a hot oven until the oysters are brought to a boiling point. Serve with one-half lemon.—*A. J. Fink, Managing Director, Southern Hotel, Baltimore.*

PANNED OYSTERS

(4 persons)

1 pint oysters, 2 tablespoons butter, ½ cup cream. Season with salt and pepper. Put butter in sauté pan, when hot add oysters. Cook until edges begin to curl, then add cream, salt and pepper. Serve on toast in platters.—*Mr. H. R. Bowen, Chesapeake Steamship Company, Baltimore.*

CHESAPEAKE LINE

PICKLED OYSTERS

One hundred large oysters, one pint white vinegar, one dozen blades of mace, two dozen whole cloves, two dozen whole black peppers, one large red pepper broken into bits. Put the oysters and their liquor into a porcelain kettle, salt to taste. Heat slowly until the oysters are very hot but not to boiling. Take them out with a skimmer and set aside to cool. To the liquor remaining in kettle add the vinegar and spices, boil up fairly and when the oysters are almost cold pour the mixture over them scalding hot. Cover the jar in which they are, put away in a cool place. Next day put the oysters into glass jars with tight tops.

Keep in the dark and where they will keep cool. If you open a jar use the contents as soon as practicable. The air like the light will turn them dark.—*Mrs. T. Rowland Thomas, Baltimore.*

OYSTER PIE

Line a pie plate with flaky pie crust. Fill with oysters seasoned with salt and pepper, dot with butter, add a few pieces of diced celery, dust with flour and add top crust.

Bake in quick oven.—*Mrs. Nell C. Westcott, Kent County.*

HAM AND PANNED OYSTERS ON TOAST

Serve a full slice of toast with a thin cut from the horseshoe part of the ham. This is to be either broiled or fried and placed on top of the toast. Serve six panned oysters nicely arranged on top of this. Serve on a tea plate, under glass cover, garnished with a cream sauce.—*Dining Car Service, B. & O. R. R.*

OYSTER LOAF

Cut an oblong slice from the upper crust of a Vienna loaf of bread. Then scoop out the crumbs from the inside. Spread the casing with butter, fill with raw oysters, about one quart. Add a tablespoonful of chopped parsley, ½ cup cream, plenty of butter, pepper, salt and two drops of Tabasco sauce. Put on upper crust. Put in baking dish and pour oyster liquor over it. Cover and bake 20 minutes, basting often with the liquor. Slice and serve hot.—*Mrs. Irving Adams, Howard County.*

"What is Francis Scott Key's greatest distinction?"
"What?"
"He knew all four verses of the 'Star-Spangled Banner.'"

PICKLED OYSTERS

Strip ½ gallon of oysters through the fingers. After straining their liquor through a piece of thin muslin put it on the fire and when it comes to a boil put the oysters in and let them come to a boil. Then take the oysters out of this hot liquor and throw them in cold water. Strain this liquor from which the hot oysters have been taken, then add one teaspoon each of whole mace, whole allspice, and whole white pepper. Let this come to a boil and after taking the oysters out of the cold water pour this boiling hot water over them adding one cup of cold vinegar.—*Mrs. Caroline A. Tyler, Baltimore (Courtesy Mrs. Samuel T. Earle).*

OYSTER FRITTERS

Take out oysters from shell, drain off the juice, salt and pepper oysters. Make egg batter, using oyster juice to thin batter. Do not thin too much. Mix batter well, then stir in oysters and fry in deep fat.—*Mr. H. N. Busick, Managing Director, Lord Baltimore Hotel, Baltimore.*

PICKLED OYSTERS

Strain the liquor from one gallon of oysters, put the oysters on a towel and wipe them dry by putting another towel on top of them. Take 1½ pts. of their liquor, add 1 small pt. vinegar, 1 heavy tablespoon salt, 1 heavy tablespoon cloves (whole), 1 heavy tablespoon allspice (whole), 1 heavy tablespoon pounded white ginger, 1 heavy tablespoon mace (whole), 10 whole white peppers. Let come to a boil, throw in the oysters, when the gills curl, take them off and cover in a stone jar.—*Mrs. E. Glenn Perine, Baltimore.*

SHELL OYSTER ROAST

Select eight large shell oysters and wash well. Lay them in a frying pan and set in a very hot oven for about ten minutes, when the oysters begin to open, serve them on the shell, place on a folded napkin upon a dinner plate. Cut a strip of bacon in two pieces, laying one small piece on each oyster, with parsley and half a lemon. Serve the liquor from the oysters with melted butter (*hot*), separate in a gravy boat.—*Dining Car Service, B. & O. R. R.*

GRILLED OYSTERS, BALTIMORE

Dry one dozen large oysters on a towel, sprinkle with pepper, dip same in drawn butter and fresh bread crumbs, broil quickly to a light golden color. Cover two pieces of toast with two slices of Maryland cured ham (broiled), place six oysters on each piece of ham, garnish top with slice of lemon and sprig of parsley and pour around it a light cream sauce with chopped celery cooked into it.—*A. J. Fink, Managing Director, Southern Hotel, Baltimore.*

FANCY ROAST OYSTERS

Scrub shells until clean, arrange in baking pan and place in very hot oven until the shells open, remove the flat shell and loosen oyster from deep shell. Place a little melted butter in each and serve while hot.—*Hotel Rennert, Baltimore.*

OYSTER STEW

(For one)

Two teaspoonsful butter, one teaspoon flour, one cup of rich milk, five to eight oysters, depending on size, salt and pepper, and a few drops of Worcestershire sauce.

Melt butter, add flour and blend well, being careful not to let it burn. Add milk and stir until smooth and boiling. Now add oysters with a little of their juice, being careful that no bits of shell cling to them. Let come to a boil again, cooking just a few seconds—until the edges of the oysters curl. Serve at once.—*Mrs. Alice K. Wilcox, Tudor Hall Inn, St. Mary's County.*

SCALLOPED OYSTERS

Wash and drain one pint of medium oysters. Have ready a deep baking dish, place a layer of oysters in the bottom, then a layer of cracker crumbs. Pour over them a little of the oyster liquor. Then a layer of oysters, then another of crumbs. Continue until dish is filled. Dot each layer with butter, and salt and pepper to taste. Bake in oven until brown.—*Mrs. J. B. Tawes, Somerset County.*

OYSTER STEW

1 quart oysters, ½ cup milk and a little cream, 2 tablespoons butter, 2 tablespoons flour, a little finely chopped celery with tops, salt, pepper to taste. Drain oysters through a colander for an hour or more. Then hold colander under cold water spigot and run the water, washing the oysters in the hands. Drain for a few minutes so that they will be free of water. Put the oysters in a saucepan and add the clear liquor that has been drained from the oysters. Put on stove with milk, salt, pepper and celery and cook until the oysters' gills curl, then add butter and flour which has been mixed by melting the butter and stirring the flour in it. Lastly add cream, the more the richer.

OYSTER SOUP

Use the same receipt, adding more milk and a dash of mace mixed with flour.—*Readbourne Receipts, Queen Anne's County (Courtesy of Misses Clara and Bessie Hollyday).*

"OYEEE, OYEEE—E——E"

TERRAPIN

TERRAPIN

COOKING terrapin is like making corn bread or curing and cooking ham, there simply is no receipt that is sufficient. Almost everybody uses the same formal directions, similar to those used at the Maryland and Baltimore Clubs, or the Rennert Hotel, but they are only a general guide. Just as one can watch carefully day after day a good cook make rolls or pastry but never be able to make them right one's self, so with terrapin, experience and the cook really make the dish.

I have always thought that most receipts leave out things that are as important as the directions they contain. For instance, the careful selection of freshly caught terrapin, not too large and not too old; a great deal of care in picking them and the discard of much of the meat that is commonly used, including most of the white meat because only a small part of this is tender and has any flavor; and then the cooking and gradual seasoning in the chafing dish, almost entirely a thing of tasting and many previous cookings.

At times sherry wine is added just before the terrapin is served, or even after it has reached the individual plates, but this is not the manner of the true lover of terrapin. Wine, sherry or Madeira according to one's taste, is an essential accompaniment but it should not be added as a flavor.

The final flavor of the dish is almost as elusive as the shades of a delicate color and the most skillful cooks at times miss it. Although a tedious and troublesome food to prepare, in Maryland, at least, it seems to have been the one dish that always had the attention of the lady of the household. For her labors in its preparation, and for the pleasures she has given to those who like to dine well, she is justly entitled to the homage that has been paid her and the appreciation she has received.—*Daniel M. Henry, Talbot County.*

DIAMOND-BACK TERRAPIN, MARYLAND STYLE

(THIS *is the receipt used by Thornton Rollins, founder of the famous Lobby Club. Probably no terrapin served in Baltimore was wider heralded than this. A club which met but once annually, it came into existence about* 1888—*a terrapin banquet at the home of Commodore Rollins as a natural sequence to a convivial stag party at the theater. The membership was composed only of the contemporary bon-vivants de luxe, epicures and gourmets. Naught but terrapin and champagne has ever been served. The names of John T. Ford, Albert Marbury, Albert Gorter, Davies Warfield, George Cator, Columbus O'Donnell Lee, Ned Jackson, as well as the earlier members, John S. Bullock, Tom Wilkenson, Jacob Frey, Findlay Burns, Frank Krems, W. A. Boyd, William Burns and Robert Jones, are all reminiscent to the older generation of Baltimoreans of those days when the success of a terrapin dinner was not supposed, legally, to depend on those beverages that are now purported to taste "positively illegal." Today Commodore Rollins—founder and last survivor of the famous Lobby Club—is a figure loved, respected and honored by all who revere the fine art of living as practiced during the last century in Baltimore.*)

Immerse live terrapin in boiling water and boil under cover until tender or when feet crush easily by pinching. Then withdraw from water, placing each terrapin on its back in order to retain the natural essence. When cool remove yellow shell skin. Use all meat portions, eggs and liver. Be careful not to let any of the gall bladder penetrate the meat or essence. To each six inch terrapin use one quarter pound of butter and one-half cup of good sherry wine. Salt and red pepper to taste.—*Commodore Thornton Rollins, Baltimore.*

DIAMOND-BACK TERRAPIN

Place live terrapin in boiling water for about three minutes, remove and by pulling out head and feet, the skin with rough towel and clip off claws from feet with shears.

Replace terrapin in enough boiling water to cover, and boil slowly for from one to two hours, according to size. Terrapin is cooked when meat may be removed from bones. Take from water and let cool only enough to be handled—it should be kept warm for the following operation.

Break the legs and joints, discarding the intestines. Slice liver in small pieces, being careful not to break the gall which must be removed from liver, take out the eggs, wash same carefully and set aside until ready to serve.

Reduce the broth terrapin has been cooked in, by boiling, into a strong jelly and pour over terrapin enough to cover entirely.

The preparation arrived at so far may be divided into portions desired, and, if put in glass jars and kept in refrigerator, covered with sweet butter to keep air tight, will keep for several days until ready to finish and serve in the following manner.

Place portion to be served in chafing dish or pan, add half pound of sweet butter to one quart of terrapin meat. Flavor with salt and pepper (cayenne) to suit taste, add eggs and when nice and creamy serve boiling hot. If Sherry is desired, same may be added before serving.—*Maryland Club, Baltimore.*

TERRAPIN

Place the terrapin in boiling water, let cook until in lifting by hind leg the body of terrapin separates from it. Let it cool, remove the entrails, carefully remove the gall from the liver, and place it with the entrails. Pick the terrapin, disjointing the bones. Make a dressing of butter, salt, black pepper and a dash of cayenne to taste. Recook in chafing dish or double boiler, and serve hot. A dash of sherry in serving is sometimes desired.

34

This receipt is intended only for first-class Chesapeake Bay Diamond Back terrapin, each of which if measuring 6 inches should weigh not less than 2 pounds.—*General Francis E. Waters, Baltimore.*

DIAMOND-BACK TERRAPIN

Throw terrapin in water and let them be cleansed from all dirt—about one hour. Plunge into boiling water for ten minutes, remove and take off toe nails, rubbing off the skin from shell, head, neck and legs.

Put into fresh boiling water and cook until tender (the legs). When done set off to cool and open the shell. Detach meat from shell, being careful to remove the stomach and gall bladder, which are thrown away, also lower intestines. Cut up all other parts into small pieces, allowing ½ pound of butter to a terrapin. Season with salt, cayenne pepper and ½ gill of sherry to each terrapin. Only use water the terrapin is last cooked in for essence. —*Mrs. T. Rowland Thomas, Baltimore.*

SEA FOOD

SEA FOOD

ONE of Maryland's major scenic glories, the Chesapeake Bay, is also the source of some of her greatest gastronomic delights. This body of water, together with its many estuaries, has from the earliest days of the Maryland Colony generously provided her citizens with food and a means of livelihood.

The Chesapeake oyster is known the length and breadth of the country, particularly those varieties designated as "Tangiers" and "Chincoteagues." The former, while diminishing somewhat in quantity, is still supreme in quality, and the "Chincoteague," so called from the fact that it is caught in Chincoteague Bay, on the seaside, is considered by many to be the best raw oyster marketed. Certain it is that the sea, which salts this inland bay of Maryland, gives the Chincoteague its very special "tang." But the oysters from other sections of Chesapeake Bay also have their champions; the Potomac River oyster is popular, and those coming from Patuxent River were great favorites in the days of the "raw bar." Maryland even has its "green" oyster, a bivalve similar in aspect to the famous Marennes oyster so highly prized by the French. This oyster does not, however, possess the "coppery" flavor which characterizes the French oyster, although it has valuable properties and is recommended in the treatment of anemia cases.

In addition to the oyster, Chesapeake Bay is the natural habitat of the blue crab, which is wholly delicious, either in its hard or soft shell states. Maryland soft crabs with tartar sauce are to be found on reputable menus everywhere from May until November, and the meat of the hard crab is equally pleasing, whether one eats it cold in a salad, or hot in such varied forms as deviled or imperial crabs, crab flakes au gratin, or even, and perhaps to many, *especially,* as the old-fashioned steamed crab. In this last form, the crab is eaten wholly with the fingers, and plenty of leisure and informal attire are recommended. In an earlier day, cold and foamy beer was (*and still should be*) the proper accompaniment for steamed crabs.

As if the crab and the oyster were not enough to shed luster on the Chesapeake, a number of varieties of very fine fish, which inhabit these waters, should be specifically mentioned. Foremost among them, although it is not in the strict sense of the word a native, but visits us only in the spring when it seeks the brackish waters of the upper Bay for spawning, is the shad. Both the fish and its eggs are highly esteemed, but the former has the distinct disadvantage of possessing a multiplicity of bones. It has been stated that shad, if boiled for five minutes before being prepared for baking, can be boned as readily as other fish.

First in importance among the native fishes of the Chesapeake is the striped bass, or rock, as it is commonly called. Firm and fine of texture, the meat of the striped bass is delicious in any of the many ways recommended for its preparation. Trolling for this fish is one of the major sports of the Chesapeake, and literally thousands of fishermen engage in it during the summer and early autumn months. Blue fish, sea trout, croakers (commonly called hardheads), perch and large-mouth black bass are found in abundance in the waters of the Bay and its tributaries. The inland or non-tidal waters teem with brook, rainbow and brown trout, small mouth bass and many other varieties of fresh-water fishes.

Last, because of its comparative scarcity only, must be mentioned the diamond-back terrapin of Maryland. This amphibian, once so plentiful in the Chesapeake Bay country that it was a common food for the poor and slaves, is now in the luxury class. Among a generation accustomed to the fine Madeira so necessary to the proper preparation of terrapin, this dish, coming after the soup, was the beginning of every important dinner. All efforts to raise the diamond-back terrapin in captivity have been comparatively unsuccessful, so the present "natural" crop brings fantastically high prices. In a generation devoted to slenderizing diets, perhaps the terrapin will not be missed, but among epicures, regretful sighs are the proper accompaniment to a discussion of the diamond-back.—*Swepson Earle.*

(MR. SWEPSON EARLE *as Conservation Commissioner for the State of Maryland deserves no end of credit for his success in developing the game resources of the State, not only marine game but wild fowl and fur-bearing animals as well. Oysters, crabs, fish, duck, deer, wild turkey, field game, trout stream and lake all receive his attention and sportsmen from the mountains of Garrett County, up and down the length of the great Chesapeake and across to Chincoteague Bay rely on his resourcefulness for a good season's sport. Keenly alert to the benefits of the most modern scientific research in Conservation development, the new marine laboratory at Solomon's Island is one of the best equipped in the country and was installed upon his recommendation and under his direct supervision. He is author of "The Chesapeake Bay Country," which has brought the interest in this remarkable body of water into nearly every civilized country. Considering that he is keeper, and protector of Maryland's wild life, which contributes so much to the gastronomic superiority of the Maryland Free State, he may well be considered one of the most important cogs in its governmental machinery.*)

CRAB CAKES

1 lb. crab meat, 1 cup bread crumbs, 1 egg, 1 teaspoonful mustard, salt and pepper to taste. Form in cakes and fry quickly in deep fat.—*Mrs. Nell C. Westcott, Kent County.*

"I don't like the looks of this 'ere 'addock."
"Well, if it's looks ye're after, lydy, ye'd do better by the goldfish!"

SMOTHERED CAT FISH

(Bayou Inn *is situated on what was formerly known as Concord Point. It was on this point that the battery was located that repulsed the British Fleet during the attack on Havre de Grace, May 3, 1813. At the very head of the great Chesapeake Bay it is possible to see many miles to the south as well as across to the "Eastern Sho'." The view is one of the finest on the bay and in season the country in the immediate vicinity is a sportsman's paradise for migratory waterfowl and fish. One of the four famous race courses of Maryland, that of Havre de Grace, is "just around the corner" from Bayou Inn and during the racing season it is a Mecca for all ardent followers of the "sport of kings.")*

Select one large cat fish. Skin and place in baking pan. Slice onions and place on top of fish with strips of bacon. Sift flour, light pepper, and salt to season. Place in heated oven fifteen minutes. Ready to serve with waffles.—*Hotel Bayou, Harford County.*

FRIED CLAMS

Open as many clams as needed to serve. Grind or cut them in small pieces. Add one beaten egg, salt, pepper and flour enough to make a medium batter. ½ teaspoonful of yeast powder (baking powder) should be added.

Fry on griddle in hot grease.—*Mrs. J. B. Tawes, Somerset County.*

BAKED CRAB FLAKES

Cream together four tablespoonsful of butter and two tablespoonsful of flour.

Heat thoroughly in a double boiler, two cups milk (not boiling), add flour and butter, stirring constantly. Cook until creamy. Remove from fire and stir in one egg well beaten.

Mash one hard-boiled egg, mince a little parsley and add with salt and red pepper to sauce. Then add two pounds of crab flakes and put in baking dish, cover with bread crumbs and bake until brown.—*Mrs. John P. Caspar, Washington County.*

SEA BASS SAUTÉ MEUNIÈRE

Take sea bass, weighing about one pound, clean and dry in towel, cut off fins and tail; leave head on, sprinkle with salt and pepper and roll lightly in flour, fry in butter till light brown, allow about eight (8) minutes for each side. Remove to platter, squeeze some lemon juice over and finely chopped parsley. Put a little butter in pan and when light brown pour over fish and serve very hot.—*Maryland Yacht Club, Baltimore.*

CLAM FRITTERS

Take six nice fresh clams, chop them in small pieces, add one cup flour, two eggs, ½ cup milk, ½ oz. salt, two pinches ground white pepper, ½ oz. baking powder, mix well. Have a skillet with ¼ pint of good oil very hot, and make with a large soup spoon full four or five cakes in the hot oil, let it fry for four minutes on each side.—*Charles Bitterli, Chef de Cuisine, Hotel Emerson, Baltimore.*

CRAB CAKES BALTIMORE

Take one pound of crab meat for each four crab cakes. Put crab meat into mixing bowl, add one and one-half teaspoons salt, one teaspoon white pepper, one teaspoon English dry mustard and two teaspoons Worcestershire sauce, one yolk of egg and one soup spoon cream sauce or mayonnaise, one teaspoon chopped parsley. Mix well, making four crab cakes, press hard together, dip into flour, then into beaten eggs, then into bread crumbs. Fry them in hot grease pan.—*Mr. H. N. Busick, Managing Director, Lord Baltimore Hotel, Baltimore.*

CREAMED CLAMS

Chop two dozen clams very fine. Cook them slowly in a little boiling water. Add beaten yolks of two eggs, a dash of cayenne pepper, one cup of milk and enough flour to slightly thicken mixture. Let all cook together for one minute. Add teaspoonful of chopped parsley and pour over buttered toast.—*Mrs. Ida Kenney, Baltimore.*

CLAM PIE (INDIVIDUAL)

One cup thinly sliced potatoes parboiled; six clams chopped fine. Place layer of potatoes in chicken pie dish, then layer of clams, sprinkle over this one teaspoon minced onion. Continue until dish is filled. Beat one egg into half a cup of milk and pour over the contents of the chicken pie dish. Make a biscuit crust to cover the pie and bake for thirty minutes. Serve hot.—*Dining Car Service, B. & O. R. R.*

PLANKED ROCK BASS

(4 persons)

Broil bass first. Place on plank with garniture of potatoes, then place in oven until potatoes brown. Add fried oysters, scallops, fried tomatoes, Canadian bacon and cold slaw salad.—*John R. Folger, The Belvedere, Baltimore.*

CRAB FLAKE IN CASSEROLE

Two pounds crab flake, pick over and remove shell, add one pint of milk and let come to a boil in a double boiler. Cream four heaping tablespoons of butter with two of flour, add salt and pinch of red pepper. Add this to milk just before it boils, let it thicken, then cool. Add one beaten egg. Have two hard-boiled eggs mashed with fork and add to the above with a little chopped parsley and two teaspoons of sherry wine. Stir this mixture into the crab flakes and pour into the casserole. Add bread crumbs on top and bake in a quick oven about twenty minutes.—*Mrs. Robert E. Tubman, Glasgow, Dorchester County.*

CRAB FLAKE CUTLETS

(Two pounds of Flakes will make about 12 or 15 cutlets by these directions)

Fry an onion chopped very fine in about two ounces of butter until it is of a golden brown color; stir in about a cup of flour, or more if necessary, until it has been well mixed with melted butter. Then pour in white stock in which has boiled one onion, small carrot, a little sweet marjoram or thyme, stirring well and constantly until sauce hardens or gets stiff. Season with salt and pepper, white or cayenne (cayenne better), and chopped parsley. Stir this mixture into the crab meat, and put aside to cool; afterwards shape and egg; then roll in bread crumbs and fry in hot fat.

HOLLANDAISE SAUCE

Heat in saucepan a slice of onion, bay leaf, little chopped celery or celery seed and two tablespoons vinegar, two ounces butter. Stir in two tablespoons of flour to thicken, then moisten with chicken stock. Mix well. Add a little nutmeg, and salt. Cook for about thirty minutes. Beat yolks of three eggs separately with juice of half lemon. Pour into sauce but do not boil again. Rub through fine sieve into serving bowl.—*Miss Mary McDaniel, Talbot County.*

HARD CRABS

Be sure that all shell is removed. Spread crab meat out in large dish and mix well in the following order: little red pepper, salt, plenty of butter and a little milk to keep it from getting too dry.

Pack back into shell of crab and cover with cracker crumbs. Bake until a golden brown. Decorate with parsley.—*Miss Mary W. Crisfield, Somerset County.*

CREAMED CRAB FLAKES

(6 persons)

Remove meat from shell of one boiled crab. Place in pan with two teaspoonsful of flour, allowing it to become hot. Add one pint of boiling milk and one-quarter pint hot cream. Stir well and boil for ten minutes. Season with salt and cayenne pepper, then add one and a half pounds of crab meat.—*Hotel Rennert, Baltimore.*

CRAB FLAKE MARYLAND

(4 persons)

(ALTHOUGH *one of the more recent hotels of the past two decades, the Emerson, built by a native son whose name it bears, epitomized in its "Chesapeake Room" the traditions of Maryland sea food and Maryland game.*)

1 lb. lump crab flakes, 1 pint milk, ½ pint cream, ¼ lb. butter, ½ oz. salt, 1 pinch cayenne pepper, 1 glass sherry wine, 2 tablespoons flour. Melt half the butter in sauce-pan, add the flour and make the cream sauce with the heated milk, set aside to keep it hot. Heat the rest of the butter in a sauce-pan, add the crab meat and fry a little, try not to break up the lumps, add salt, pepper, cream sauce and cream. Let boil for two or three minutes, then add the sherry wine, mix well. Make sure that it doesn't boil. Serve very hot in chafing dish with toast.—*Charles Bitterli, Chef de Cuisine, Hotel Emerson, Baltimore.*

47

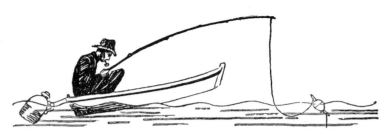

IMPERIAL DEVILED CRAB

Simmer the flakes of two crabs and half a chopped onion in butter, season with salt and cayenne pepper, add two cups of thick cream sauce, a dash of Worcestershire sauce, a teaspoonful of English mustard, a little chopped chives, bring to a boil and bind with the yolks of two eggs. Add a little green and Spanish pepper chopped fine. Fill crab shells, spread a little French mustard and a sprinkle of bread crumbs over the top. Place a small piece of butter on each and bake in the oven until brown. Serve with lemon.—*Hotel Rennert, Baltimore.*

CASSEROLETTE OF CRAB MEAT

Fry lumped crab meat with green and red peppers cut fine. Thicken with light rich cream sauce, season to taste, pour into casserolette only two-thirds full. Fry in butter a slice of tomato one-third of an inch thick. Set tomato on top of crab meat, then a layer of lobster over tomato and cover the whole with a Mornay sauce (to make Mornay sauce:—melt butter, add cream and cream sauce and dash of lemon; stir until as thick as batter) and glacé.—*A. J. Fink, Managing Director, Southern Hotel, Baltimore.*

CRAB MEAT DEWEY

Take one pound of crab meat, melt two ounces of butter and blend with two ounces of sifted flour, gradually add 2/3 cup of chicken stock and a pint of thin cream.

Bring to boil for about five minutes, season with salt and cayenne pepper. Stir in the yolks of three well-beaten eggs.

Pay attention that sauce is perfectly smooth, add one cup full of thin sliced cooked mushrooms and crab meat. Serve on toast in shallow casserole. Sprinkle very fine chopped parsley as garniture.—*Maryland Yacht Club, Baltimore.*

CRAB MEAT À LA CREOLE

1 pound of crab meat, 1 large green pepper, 1 medium onion, 1 thin slice ham. Cut in strips about two inches long, 1/16 inch wide; cook slowly about 10 minutes in butter till onions and

peppers are done, then add about one pound of tomatoes (skinned and seeds removed) chopped fine, and ¼ pound mushrooms sliced thin, 1 clove of crushed garlic, dampen with 3 ounces white wine, ½ pint of stock (ham if handy). Reduce same over slow fire for 10 minutes, season with salt, paprika and few grains of cayenne pepper and mix all together, serve with timbales of dry boiled rice.—*Maryland Yacht Club, Baltimore.*

CRAB FLAKES CHESAPEAKE

(*4 persons*)

(THE *Belvedere Hotel has always been regarded as one of the most substantial of the hotels of the South. The first of the modern hotels to be erected in Baltimore it has always respected its responsibility to uphold Maryland's reputation for hospitality and an excellent cuisine.*)

2 lbs. crab flakes, 1 cup cream, 16 shrimp, 2 green peppers, chopped, 8 mushrooms, ½ teaspoonful paprika, ½ teaspoonful salt, 2 tablespoonfuls butter, 1 glass sherry wine. Cook crab flakes in cream. Add shrimp, green peppers chopped, mushrooms, paprika, also one glass sherry wine.—*John R. Folger, Manager, The Belvedere, Baltimore.*

SOFT CRABS

Twelve small crabs, one-half pound butter, black pepper, salt, flour. See that crabs are cleaned thoroughly, wash and wipe dry, salt and season highly with black pepper, then dust with flour. Have butter at boiling point, put crabs in pan, and turn frequently until nicely browned. Serve at once, garnished with parsley and tartar sauce.—*Mrs. R. E. Bradley, Sr., Baltimore.*

"SAWF CRABS, SAWF CRABS"

DEVILED CRABS

1 lb. crab meat, 12 clean crab shells, ½ teaspoonful black pepper, ¼ teaspoonful red pepper, 1 teaspoonful salt, 1 tablespoonful butter, 1 cup milk, 1 tablespoonful flour. Put into a saucepan one tablespoonful of butter and melt. Add to it, stirring smoothly, one tablespoonful of flour and one cup of milk. Cook until it thickens. Add crab meat and seasoning and blend together. Fill crab shells, dip the tops of the filled shells in beaten egg, then cracker meal, and brown in hot oven.—*Mrs. I. P. Horsey, Somerset County.*

FISH TIMBALE

One and a half pounds of raw, white fish, mashed through colander. One and a half pint double cream, small piece of butter, four eggs, juice of small onion, pepper and salt.

Add cream to fish, beating all the time, then well-beaten yolks and whites (stiff), seasoning, butter. Sprinkle a china mold with flour, pour in mixture and bake half an hour in oven in hot water pan. Eat with:—

Oyster Sauce: Make a rich cream gravy and add one-half pint chopped oysters, season and pour over Fish Timbale.—*Miss Louisa Ogle Thomas, Baltimore.*

LOBSTER CUTLET

Season two cupfuls of minced boiled lobster with a little white pepper, onion juice and a dash of cayenne, put one cupful of cream to boil, rub smoothly together one large tablespoon of butter and three of flour and stir into the cream, stir over the fire until it forms a thick paste, then add the beaten yolks of two eggs, cook a moment and take from the fire, adding the lobster. Mix well, add a tablespoonful of chopped parsley—when cold, form into cutlets—beat an egg thoroughly and add a tablespoon of boiling water, dip cutlets into this and bread crumbs and fry in hot lard. Serve with yellow sauce.—*Dr. Walter Forman Wickes, Wickcliffe, Greenspring Valley, Baltimore County.*

"HARDHEADS," "GROWLERS," OR "CROAKERS"

Take head off, split fish. Take out backbone. Sprinkle with salt and then sift over with flour or meal, drop in hot skillet in about one inch of cooking oil. Do not immerse. Skillet and oil must be hot before placing fish on to cook. Cook slowly. Care must be taken in turning fish, use wide cake turner. Fish should be flesh side down at first, and only turned once.—*W. T. Emory, Manager, Log Inn, On the Chesapeake, Annapolis.*

LOBSTER THERMIDOR

Boil lobster for 15 to 18 minutes. Then split in two. Remove the meat and cut in small pieces. Remove the meat from the claws also. Add mushrooms in same size, sauté in butter for few minutes, and add pinch dry mustard and little paprika. Mix with

53

Bearnaise sauce. Refill the shell and put under the broiler until brown.

To make Bearnaise sauce, take 2 egg yolks for each half lb. butter. Put the egg yolks in a copper pan; add one or two table-spoonsful water and crushed pepper. Then place the copper pan in a larger pan half full of water to boiling point. Beat constantly until it begins to get thick. Add melted butter very slowly and keep beating. After this is done, flavor with tarragon vinegar and juice of one or half lemon. Strain through a cheesecloth.—*Mr. Ivan W. Poling, Manager, Fort Cumberland Hotel, Allegany County.*

BROILED FRESH MACKEREL—ANCHOVY BUTTER

(THE *Maryland Yacht Club situated on the finest and most complete yacht basin in the country is unique in its advantages to owners of watercraft. Although within the limits of the City of Baltimore it has the entire Chesapeake Bay and its many tributaries for a playground. It is only natural that its cuisine should be noted for sea-food dishes, much of which are caught within one hour's cruise of the Club.*)

Split mackerel and bone for broiling, season with salt and pepper and dip in oil. Lay skin side down on broiler and cook under moderate fire until browned. If fish is not too large it is only necessary to cook on flesh side. Remove to hot platter and spread with previously prepared butter.

Anchovy Butter

Remove skin and bones from two ounces of anchovies, dry thoroughly and pound in mortar to a paste. Add ½ ounce anchovy paste and pound till thoroughly mixed, then work in ¼ pound of good butter and pass through a fine sieve. Keep in ice box until needed.—*Maryland Yacht Club, Baltimore.*

54

THE MARYLAND YACHT CLUB

BOILED ROCK WITH EGG SAUCE

Cover fish with water, one slice of onion, two slices of lemon, add salt water and boil until done. Pour over, egg sauce and chopped parsley.—*Hotel Rennert, Baltimore.*

BOILED ROCK FISH

After the fish is clean, wrap in a cloth that has been scalded and dipped in cold water. Wrap the fish up well and drop in boiling water. Cook slowly for twenty minutes. The fish should weigh four pounds.—*Mrs. Charles Wickes Whaland, M.D., Kent County.*

THE PLAINS

("THE PLAINS," *so called because of the level ground between Indian and Trent Hall Creeks on which it is located. It was built quite some time before the Revolution and has remained in the Sothoron family ever since. It still carries the marks of a conflict between the British Fleet and a company of Maryland Militia stationed there to prevent the Britishers from proceeding farther.*)

MANINOSE

Along the crescent-shaped shore of this old home, during the winter months, when low tides often come, there can be found buried quite near the surface a shellfish very like a clam, though a softer shell and very easily opened. To cook these maninose in a hot pan with a little butter, for they are quite rich, makes a most delicious morsel, quite unlike any other shellfish in flavor, and gives variety to the winter diet of this remote home.—*Mrs. John H. Sothoron, The Plains, St. Mary's County.*

"FRESH FEESH, FRESH FEESH!"

DEVILED CRAB

(4 persons)

1 cup crab meat, ½ cup milk, ⅛ teaspoon dry mustard, ¼ teaspoon cayenne pepper, ½ green pepper chopped fine, 1 cup bread crumbs, yolks of 2 raw eggs, 1 teaspoon salt, ½ cup melted butter. Mix crab meat with crumbs (which have been moistened with milk) and egg yolks. Add mustard, salt, cayenne pepper, green peppers and butter. Mix well. Fill crab shells with mixture, sift crumbs lightly on top, dot with butter. Brown quickly in very hot oven, being careful they do not burn. Crab shells should be washed and scrubbed in very hot water before being stuffed.—*Mr. H. R. Bowen, Chesapeake Steamship Company, Baltimore.*

LOBSTER MARYLAND STYLE

Cut cooked lobsters in slices one-quarter inch in thickness, sauté in fresh butter, moisten with cream, let simmer for a few minutes, and before serving thicken the lobster with cooked yolks of eggs, crush with double the amount of butter, then press through a fine sieve, seasoning with red and white pepper and add a little good sherry.—*Mr. H. N. Busick, Managing Director, Lord Baltimore Hotel, Baltimore.*

SOFT CRABS

Cleanse crabs by removing spongy substance under pointed flap at either side. Remove pointed piece underneath called the apron. Cut straight across the front to remove eyes and sandbag. Sprinkle *very lightly* with salt and then with flour. Have oil in pan moderately hot and not deep. *Do not immerse.* When brown on one side turn and brown. Time:—about twenty minutes, or according to size of crab. Serve with tartar sauce.—*W. T. Emory, Manager, Log Inn, On the Chesapeake, Annapolis.*

BAKED SHAD

Take off the head, and without cutting open, draw and clean the fish, stuff with dry stale bread crumbs, into which has been mixed one onion, cut this and fry in butter; two ounces butter, salt, pepper and one teaspoonful each of nutmeg, parsley, and the well-beaten yolks of two eggs. Salt and pepper the fish, put in a baking pan with a little water, and bake until done.—*Mrs. E. W. Humphreys, Wicomico County.*

First deaf farmer to a second deaf farmer who is carrying fishing paraphernalia:
"Howdy, goin' fishin'?"
SECOND DEAF FARMER: *"No, goin' fishin'."*
FIRST DEAF FARMER: *"Is that so? I thought maybe you were goin' fishin'."*

SHAD ROE CROQUETTES

Simmer shad roe fifteen minutes in 1 quart of boiling water, with 1 teaspoon of salt, 1 tablespoon of butter, 3 tablespoons of flour, ½ pint of cream or milk, 1 teaspoon of lemon juice, 1 tablespoon of chopped parsley (if desired).

Heat cream to boiling point in double boiler, cream butter and flour, add to milk. Stir on the fire until it thickens and add yolks of 2 eggs. Take from fire and add salt, add lemon juice and parsley after you take from fire. Add shad roe which has been drained from all juice. Place it in a cool place. When thor-

59

oughly chilled mold into chops. Take 1 egg, beat about 6 strokes, add 1 tablespoon of boiling water and mix thoroughly. Dip chop first into egg. Cover well with egg and dip it into the bread crumbs until every spot is covered, and then fry in boiling lard or olive oil, 2 tablespoons of oil for a dozen. Cotton seed oil may be used.—*John Ridgely, of Hampton, Baltimore County.*

STEWED SNAPPER

Secure one good-sized snapper. It must be killed the day before it is to be cooked. After the snapper has been thoroughly bled, wash it well in cold water; throw it into boiling water, boil fifteen minutes.

Take it from the water, separate the upper and under shells carefully, keeping your knife close to the shell and remove the meat entire. Open carefully, remove the bladder and intestines. Cut the gall carefully from the liver. Saw or break the shell, put in the bottom of the kettle, place the meat on top, cover with one quart of boiling water; add two bay leaves, one onion sliced, four cloves, a few whole peppercorns, or a salt spoonful of white pepper.

Cover and simmer gently for one and a half hours or until the meat is tender. Cut the meat into dices, using one-half the liver. Rub together one tablespoonful of butter and one of flour; add the meat, stir until boiling and add a teaspoonful of Kitchen Bouquet and a level teaspoonful of salt and the meat. Cut into slices two hard-boiled eggs and half of a lemon. Put this into a tureen with six tablespoonsful of Madeira or sherry; pour over and serve.—*D. Charles Winebrener, Frederick County.*

"——and a single shad will have two thousand baby shad."
"Goodness, and how many do the married ones have?"

STUFFED SHAD ROE, FOUNTAIN INN

(THE *site of the Southern Hotel is the only one in this country that has never been used for any other purpose other than that of a hostelry. In the days before, during, and after the Revolution, Fountain Inn, which stood upon this site, was frequently visited by George Washington, also by the Marquis de Lafayette, the Count de Rochambeau as well as by John Adams and General Nathanael Greene. It was a rendezvous for the members of the Continental Congress when that body held its sessions in Baltimore during the winter of 1776-1777.*)

Poach shad roe with a piece of butter, salt, pepper, and a few drops of white wine. Drain roe, split without separating entirely, fill center with purée of fresh mushrooms, close same, place on thin piece of buttered toast. Prepare a Mornay sauce (to make Mornay sauce:—melt butter, add cream and cream sauce and dash of lemon; stir until as thick as batter), add to sauce puree of mushrooms equal to one-third the quantity of your sauce, pour over shad roe and glacé. Serve with ribbon of thick tomato sauce around platter and garnish with four small patty shells filled with new peas.—*A. J. Fink, Managing Director, Southern Hotel, Baltimore.*

BROILED SMELTS, MAÎTRE D'HÔTEL

Take six large smelts, split from the back to take large bones out, wash and dry, dip into olive oil and paprika, then in fresh bread crumbs. Broil under brisk fire to golden color, serve on platter with creamed maître d'hôtel butter (butter melted, with finely chopped parsley) if wanted. Add lemon and sprig of parsley.—*A. J. Fink, Managing Director, Southern Hotel, Baltimore.*

SEA FOOD IN CHAFING DISH

(4 persons)

12 scallops, 12 oysters, 12 shrimps, ½ lobster, ½ lb. crab flakes, ½ teaspoonful salt, 2 teaspoonfuls butter, 4 tablespoonfuls Hollandaise sauce, ½ cup sherry wine. Scallops, oysters, shrimp, lobster, crab flakes cooked in cream. Add salt, pepper and butter, two tablespoonfuls Hollandaise sauce and two dashes of sherry wine.—*John R. Folger, Manager, The Belvedere, Baltimore.*

FRIED NORFOLK SPOTS

Wash fish well, then allow to dry. Dip in cracker meal and flour mixed. Season with salt and pepper and fry in shallow fat. Serve with parsley and lemon.—*Hotel Rennert, Baltimore.*

TUDOR HALL

("TUDOR HALL," *Leonardtown, overlooking Breton Bay, was built about 1760 by Abram Barnes. It was bought by the family of Francis Scott Key, author of "The Star-Spangled Banner," about 1800 and has been owned by that family ever since. It has been used intermittently as an inn where one could obtain a most satisfactory repast. At such times it was open to the public. It is well worth a visit.*)

SMOTHERED ROCK FISH

For this we prefer a fish of three pounds or more. Have it scaled and cleaned but do not remove head. Place in roaster. Sprinkle with salt and pepper, in cavity and on both sides, spread over it one-half cup of chopped onion. Pour over it one-half cup of melted butter and one-half cup of hot water. Bake, covered, in hot oven, basting frequently. It will take about a half hour to cook and is done when a carving fork can pierce it easily.—*Mrs. Alice K. Wilcox, Tudor Hall Inn, St. Mary's County.*

TOURIST: *"Any trout up this way?"*
GARRETT COUNTIAN: *"Thousands of 'em."*
TOURIST: *"Bite?"*
GARRETT COUNTIAN: *"Sure! Why, they're absolutely vicious! A man has to hide behind a tree to bait his hook."*

FRIED ROCK FISH

We use the smaller fish for this—not much over a pound. After cleaning, as in receipt for Smothered Rock, dip in a beaten egg and milk—two eggs to a cup of milk—and add half a teaspoonful of salt. Then dip in fine dry crumbs. Fry until brown in fat enough to cover at 375 degrees Fahrenheit.—*Mrs. Alice K. Wilcox, Tudor Hall Inn, St. Mary's County.*

BROILED TROUT

Clean, wash and wipe dry a salmon or gray trout weighing about three pounds. Cut the head off and split the fish in two. Remove all bones. Season with salt and pepper, rub over with melted fat. Place the fish on the broiler. At the beginning the fish should be kept close to the fire to sear its surface as quickly as possible. Gradually remove the broiler to a lower position as the fish cooks, turning as needful until tender.

When done, dress on a hot platter and pour over three ounces of melted butter. Garnish with whole parsley and pieces of lemon.—*Mr. H. R. Bowen, Chesapeake Steamship Company, Baltimore.*

STEWED MARYLAND SNAPPER

1 medium size snapper, 2 cups of flour, browned, 2 quarts of turtle meat, 1 to 2 small onions and chopped celery salted in butter, salt and pepper to season, 1 teacup of good sherry wine, 3 hard-boiled eggs chopped fine, squeeze teaspoon lemon juice. —*Hotel Bayou, Harford County.*

FILET OF SOLE

(*4 persons*)

8 filets, 1 cup white wine, 2 tomatoes chopped, 6 mushrooms, chopped, 2 teaspoonfuls chives, chopped. Cooked in pan with white wine. When ready to serve cover with tomatoes, chopped mushrooms, and little chives.—*John R. Folger, Manager, The Belvedere, Baltimore.*

GAME

BEAR STEAK

(MISS ZAIDEE BROWNING *is a great-granddaughter of the famous pioneer hunts-man, Meshach Browning, whose fascinating tales and experiences of this section were published years after his death under the title of "Forty-four years of the Life of a Hunter." While I was discussing the cuisine of Western Maryland with Miss Browning, my glance fell upon a bear-skin rug of heroic proportion on the floor in front of the fireplace. I asked if it were a native product and was assured in the affirmative. It was only natural that I then request her receipt for cooking bear steak. She graciously complied.*)

I had the steak cut about an inch thick and put butter in a good hot skillet. Lay the steak in the skillet until it is seared and browned on one side; then turn and cook equally on the other side; add pepper and salt and when done apply a goodly amount of butter. There really is little difference between cooking bear steak and other steak, except care should be taken that it is sufficiently well cooked, otherwise the flavor may be too strong and gamey for the average taste.—*Miss Zaidee Browning, Garrett County.*

CANVAS BACK DUCK

(CERTAINLY *no Maryland shrine has done more to memorialize Maryland cooking than the Rennert. From the very inception of the hostelry in 1888 it has employed only colored chefs and colored waiters. For many years Mrs. Rennert herself closely supervised the food, its selection, preparation and serving. Since then the Rennert has established friendships through its food in every State in the Union. It is no longer a Maryland institution but a national one with an international reputation.*

Its oyster bar is one of the most frequented points of interest to the tourists. In its lobbies and dining rooms, one is likely to meet any Maryland statesman or politician, for many a bloodless political battle of the Maryland Free State has been settled at the Rennert across a damask cloth.)

Stuff duck with celery stalks uncut, season well with salt and pepper and bake in hot oven twenty minutes.—*Hotel Rennert, Baltimore.*

CANVAS BACK DUCK

Soak ducks 24 hours in salted water. Then lay them in fresh water for two hours. Season with salt and pepper to taste and then place in a baking pan. When half done take them out and pour brandy and wine in them. Make a little thickening with flour and put in the gravy. Put back in stove and cook until nearly done. Take out and pour more brandy and wine in them, then baste well with the gravy until thoroughly cooked nice and brown.—*Mrs. E. W. Humphreys, Wicomico County.*

WILD DUCK

The art of cooking wild duck is peculiar to different localities, but this receipt is usually used by game lovers of Maryland.

For canvas back, red head and black duck: Do not draw the

ducks more than three hours before you will use them. The less time the better. They bleed freely and should be washed in as little water as possible and with a rag, as otherwse you lose much of the blood, which of course is the flavor. Do not stuff with anything as it is important the heat should strike inside of the duck to prevent the loss of juices there. Have an old-time baking pan not higher than two inches on the sides so the heat can sear the duck at once and does not steam them, causing loss of juices. Have a very hot oven, hot enough to sear them over at once. Have the breast rubbed with butter. Put them in the low baking dish with as little water as possible, baste three times, adding boiling water to the baking dish each time so that it will not dry. Bake twenty-two minutes if you can have a very, very hot oven, or twenty-five if your oven isn't so good. This is not an exceedingly rare duck.—*Mrs. Lewin W. Wickes, Kent County.*

FROG LEGS

(MARYLAND *sea food properly cooked is all that the most exacting palate can demand. The pleasure it gives can be augmented only by indulgence within the sight of its famous origin—the great Chesapeake Bay. This may be had in most congenial surroundings at Log Inn, just around the corner from Annapolis; where one may breathe deep the aroma of the Bay blended with that of a platter of freshly cooked rock, bass or crabs prepared in the favorite manner.*)

Frogs should be served right after they are killed. After cleaning, every part of the frog but the head is used. Sprinkle flour lightly on both sides of the frog, place in skillet with one inch deep hot cooking oil. The skillet and oil must be hot before frogs are put in it. Cook until brown.—*W. T. Emory, Manager, Log Inn, On the Chesapeake, Annapolis.*

LOG INN, ON THE CHESAPEAKE

MARSH RABBIT (MUSKRAT)

Let them soak in salted water one day and night. Put them on and parboil for about fifteen minutes. Change the water and cut up. Add onion, red pepper and salt to taste and a small quantity of fat meat. Add just enough water to keep them from burning, add a little thickening to make gravy and cook until very tender.—*Mrs. E. W. Humphreys, Wicomico County.*

PARTRIDGES

Split them open, add pepper and salt and put a little butter over them. Place them in the oven to bake. When done, serve on a hot dish, add a little water to the drippings and pour over them. —*John Ridgely, Hampton, Baltimore County.*

72

PARTRIDGE

(*The Old Eastern Shore Style*)

Pick, singe, split down the back, and remove entrails. Let stand in salted water overnight. Place in a pan, season to taste and make a little thickening for the gravy. Cook until well done. Just before you take them out of the stove, stir into the gravy about two tablespoonfuls of wine.—*Mrs. E. W. Humphreys, Wicomico County.*

ENGLISH PHEASANTS

ALSO RUFFED GROUSE AND QUAIL

The following procedure applies to each of the above.

If pheasants are young, split on back and put them in a broiler with plenty of butter, salt, and pepper. Baste thoroughly with juice from dripping pan.—*Woodmont Rod and Gun Club, Woodmont, Washington County.*

RABBIT PIE, MARYLAND STYLE

(The *Lord Baltimore Hotel has established for itself the reputation for paying homage to Maryland traditions of good food properly served.*
Modern facilities and a strict attention to culinary detail do culinary credit to the establishment as the establishment does to the name it bears.)

Skin two rabbits; draw and wipe well the meat; separate at the joints, bone the shoulders and the legs, remove part of backbone and split each one in two. With the necks, bones and a few game parings, make a sauce with white wine or tarragon vinegar. Cut half a pound of bacon into small slices, put them in a sauce-

73

pan with butter and heat for five minutes while stirring, then skim, leaving the fat in the pan, add two tablespoons each of onions, shallots and mushrooms; fry together for two minutes, then add the pieces of rabbit; season highly, being sparing of the salt, and sprinkle with pulverized wild thyme. Cover the bottom of a pie dish intended for the oven with a layer of the bacon, pour into the bottom a few tablespoonsful of the prepared sauce reduced to nearly half glaze. Wet the edges of the dish, cover it with a thin band of puff paste fragments or fine foundation paste, wet this band also. Cover the whole with a flat of puff paste parings, cut off the surplus around the edge of the dish, egg over twice and cook for an hour and a quarter in a slow oven, make a hole in the top and pour in the remainder of the sauce.—*Mr. H. N. Busick, Managing Director, Lord Baltimore Hotel, Baltimore.*

PHEASANT

Split down back. Lay in salt water for a couple of hours, to which a teaspoonful of baking soda has been added. This draws out the blood and any discoloration. Wipe dry with clean cloth. Add pepper, salt and a generous piece of butter, adding two slices of breakfast bacon to be laid across the breast of each bird. Roast until well done.—*Miss Zaidee Browning, Garrett County.*

ROAST QUAIL

Pluck and draw the birds, rub a little butter over them, tie strip of bacon on breasts and roast for twenty or twenty-five minutes in hot oven.—*Mrs. Frank L. Benz, Washington County.*

WOODMONT ROD AND GUN CLUB

WILD TURKEY

(FEW *hunting clubs have as enviable a reputation as the Woodmont Rod and Gun Club. Founded many years ago by Fighting Bob Evans it has flourished until now it is probably the best known in the country. Its limited roster of membership reads as though culled from the highest ratings of Dun or Bradstreet's and a Who's Who of National Sporting Life. Many Presidents have spent their days of relaxation there with rod and gun. Deer, wild turkey, ruffed grouse, imported pheasant, partridge, woodcock, wild duck and all upland game have served to make membership in this unusual club a coveted achievement to all lovers of good sport.)*

"It is difficult to imagine a happier conjunction than the blending of the symbols when the arms of a sportsman are quartered with those of a cook. The tints of the autumnal woods reflected in the plumage of mature and lusty game are types of rich experiences and genial sentiments which flit about the sportsman's board and linger at his hearth with as gracious a fitness as that which diffuses a faint blush through the russet of a well cooked mallard's breast, and with a zest equal to the relish which lurks within a woodcock's thigh."—JOHN ALDERGROVE.

Dress turkey, and if weather is cool, hang it outside on a porch or some convenient place for six or seven days before using. If weather is warm, hang in cold storage, but do not freeze it as freezing will take away the flavor of wild turkey. Prepare stuffing with fine bread crumbs and chestnuts as follows: Boil chestnuts until mealy, and mash them up fine. Put one-half bread crumbs and half chestnuts with some butter and salt and pepper, and mix up well. Stuff the turkey with this filling. Put in oven to roast, putting plenty of butter on turkey, also some small strips of bacon. Cover same with a cloth. While roasting baste thoroughly, and when turkey is about done, take the cloth off and brown it thoroughly. Put salt and pepper on turkey with butter before starting to roast.—*Woodmont Rod and Gun Club, Woodmont, Washington County.*

BROWN FRICASSEED RABBIT

Cut up a rabbit, put in a stewpan, stew until tender. Let water boil away, add a generous lump of butter, season with salt and pepper, let brown well on all sides, add milk to nearly cover rabbit in pan, boil up for five minutes, thicken with flour and water blended until smooth, turn into platter. Delicious.—*Mrs. E. W. Humphreys, Wicomico County.*

RABBIT FRICASSEE

Cut rabbit in pieces, roll in flour and fry brown quickly with lard in hot skillet. Arrange pieces in a casserole, cover with stock made by pouring several cups of water into the pan in which the rabbit has been browning and let it come to a boil. Season with salt, pepper, a little onion and curry. Cover and bake slowly in hot oven until tender.—*Eleanor Birnie, Carroll County.*

*"Thanks, my lord, for your venison; for finer or fatter
Never ranged in a forest or smoked in a platter.
The haunch was a picture for painters to study,
The fat was so white, and the lean was so ruddy,
Tho' my stomach was sharp, I could scarce help regretting
To spoil such a delicate picture by eating."*
—GOLDSMITH, *Haunch of Venison*

VENISON

Get pure olive oil. To one pint of olive oil grate four onions, and beat up in a dish. Get the skillet very hot, and put a little butter in it to keep it from sticking. Dip the venison steaks thoroughly in the olive oil and onions. Cook quickly and turn frequently, searing the steaks medium to well done according to how liked best. If a venison roast, pour the olive oil and onions over the roast as you start to roast it. Baste it thoroughly while cooking.—*Woodmont Rod and Gun Club, Woodmont, Washington County.*

FOWL

CARVEL HALL

("CARVEL HALL" *was erected in 1763 by William Paca, signer of the Declaration of Independence and third Governor of Maryland. The name "Carvel Hall" is derived from Winston Churchill's novel "Richard Carvel" in which this house figures as the home of Dorothy Manners, a purely fictitious character. It is one of the most charming old residences of Annapolis and is situated directly opposite the Naval Academy.*)

CHICKEN IN BATTER

Two young chickens, two cupfuls of flour, three teaspoonfuls of baking powder one-half a teaspoonful of salt, pepper, two eggs, and one-half cupful of fresh milk.

Cut chickens into pieces, dip in batter and fry raw in deep

hot fat. To make the batter:—sift flour, baking powder and seasoning all together. Beat the eggs, add one-half cupful milk, and stir in the dry ingredients. Add more milk if necessary, but this batter should be quite thick. Dip one piece at a time in this batter and drop into deep hot fat.—*Albert H. McCarthy, Manager, Carvel Hall Hotel, Anne Arundel County.*

SOUTHERN FRIED CHICKEN

Select a two pound chicken. Draw and joint. Dredge each piece in flour, salt and pepper to taste, fry in hot lard until a golden brown on each side, then lower fire, put lid on and let steam until tender. Serve on hot platter, garnished with slices of lemon.—*Mrs. Harry A. Beach, Wicomico County.*

CHICKEN POTPIE

Pastry: One quart of flour, pinch of salt, pinch of sugar, one pint of cold buttermilk, one-half teaspoon soda, three teaspoons baking powder, one-half cup of butter.

Cut chicken up and stew in salt water and minced onion. Remove chicken from broth, make a thin gravy, roll pastry, cut in individual squares. Place a piece of chicken on square, then roll and place in baking pan two inches apart. Pour gravy over squares, keeping part of the gravy to pour over squares when served. Bake in a moderate oven, well done. This is the German method. It is perfectly delicious.—*Miss Margaret Lentz Miller, Garrett County.*

CHICKEN CROQUETTES

One four-pound chicken, one small onion, one bay-leaf, four whole cloves, one pair of sweetbreads and one sprig of parsley.

Put chicken on to cook in water, add onion, bay-leaf, cloves and parsley and simmer gently until meat is tender. While this is cooking prepare sweetbreads. Trim all fat and pipes off, soak fifteen minutes, drain and cover with boiling water. Add one teaspoonful of salt, stand over moderate fire for twenty minutes, but do not boil as it toughens sweetbreads. When done put into cold water for five minutes and chop very fine with silver knife. Chop chicken fine and mix with sweetbreads, *and* to every pint allow:—

One half pint milk or cream, one large tablespoonful of

83

butter, two large tablespoonsful of flour, one large tablespoonful of chopped parsley, one teaspoonful onion juice, one teaspoonful salt and one quarter teaspoonful grated nutmeg. Red and black pepper to taste.

Put milk on to boil. Rub butter and flour to smooth paste and stir into boiling milk and stir continually until very thick. Add meat and mix thoroughly. Add seasoning and put away to cool. When cold and hard form into cone-shaped croquettes. Dip first into egg and then into bread crumbs and fry in boiling oil or fat. Serve at once with sprig of parsley in top of each.—*Mrs. Emerson C. Harrington, Jr., Dorchester County.*

FRIED CHICKEN

Dredge the chicken in flour seasoned with salt and paprika, fry in plenty of lard in hot skillet, cover. When partly done pour in a little hot water. Uncover to brown.—*The Misses Reynolds, Rose Hill Manor Inn, Frederick County.*

BOILED CHICKEN WITH DRAWN BUTTER

Boil four or five pound hen until tender. Boil six eggs until hard. Make a paste of flour and butter and melt in hot milk, stirring all the while, and as it thickens add rich top of chicken soup, (a well beaten egg adds to yellow color) and stir until you have a thick creamy yellow drawn butter. Salt to taste. Pour over chicken served whole and garnish with sliced hard boiled eggs and sprigs of parsley.—*Mrs. Emerson C. Harrington, Jr., Cambridge, Dorchester County.*

"Chickens must be the best animal the Good Lord gave us. You can eat 'em before they're born and after they're dead."

CHICKEN FRICASSEE

Cut chicken in pieces, roll in flour, and fry brown quickly with lard in hot skillet. Arrange pieces in a casserole, cover with one cup of milk (or cream); and a stock made by pouring 1½ cups of water into the pan in which the chicken has been browned; and let it come to a boil. Season with salt, pepper and celery. Cover and bake slowly in oven until tender.—*Eleanor Birnie, Carroll County*.

FRICASSEE OF CHICKEN

Joint the chicken and put it on to boil with water sufficient to cover it. When tender season with pepper, salt, marjoram, parsley chopped fine and flour. To make the balls you chop meat with half the quantity of suet and crumbled bread, parsley, pepper, and salt and one egg. Make it into balls and throw in when the stew is nearly done, as they require but a short time to cook.—*Mrs. Wm. D. Poultney, Baltimore*.

85

OLD-FASHIONED FRIED CHICKEN—
MARYLAND STYLE

Put an ounce of butter in a frying pan, and add four slices of lean salt pork dipped in flour; when turned to a golden color take off the salt pork, add two and a half pounds of chicken disjointed, also dipped in milk and flour. Fry until cooked. Take off chicken, drain fat from frying pan, pour in a cup of light cream and milk, reduce to half and add one cup of light cream sauce, boil a few minutes, strain over chicken sprinkled with chopped chives and parsley, garnish with two corn fritters, two sweet potato croquettes, two slices of fried tomato and the four pieces of crisp salt pork.—*A. J. Fink, Managing Director, Southern Hotel, Baltimore.*

MARYLAND FRIED CHICKEN

Cut young chicken into pieces and rub with salt, pepper and flour. Fry in hot fat to half cover the chicken until right brown. Serve with a cream gravy and waffles.—*Albert H. McCarthy, Manager, Carvel Hall Hotel, Anne Arundel County.*

FRIED CHICKEN

Cut up chicken and roll in flour. Melt lard and butter (approximately a tablespoonful together) in skillet and permit it to get hot. Drop in pieces of chicken, season with salt and pepper and fry slowly until a golden brown. Then cover with cold water and let simmer one-half hour.—*Mr. John Charles Thomas, Baltimore.*

(JOHN CHARLES THOMAS *is one of the most universally loved of contemporary Marylanders. His voice has charmed many thousands on the concert stage, in opera, on records and over the air. Blessed with a God-given voice, he tempers it with a personality and an understanding that wins and holds admirers for him where'er he goes. It is a keen delight to hear an artist and to know instinctively that his success however great can never mar the sincerity and friendliness which he bestows so lavishly upon his audiences. However much acclaim his voice may bring him, it can never be as much as the personality and graciousness back of its merits.)*

Mr. Thomas writes, "I have no receipts which I esteem higher than those of my Mother which compose my Sunday morning breakfast when home: fried chicken, cream gravy, German fried potatoes, apple sauce, waffles and maple syrup and coffee."

CHICKEN À LA TUDOR HALL

Cut in pieces a young chicken and slices of sugar cured ham. Fry in equal parts of butter and lard. Set aside. In the same fat fry an onion and a tomato. When nearly done add a cupful of boiled rice, the chicken and the ham, and let fry together, stirring constantly. Add enough water to cover the whole and let boil slowly until done. Season with salt, pepper, bay-leaves, chopped parsley and thyme. When cooked, let dry out a little. Serve hot.—*Edwina Booth Crossman, daughter of Edwin Booth, from Tudor Hall, birthplace of Edwin Booth, Harford County.*

CHICKEN À LA MARENGO

Cut up a chicken as for frying and steam or parboil until tender. (This can be done the day before if desired.) When ready to cook, wipe dry. Heat 1 ounce of butter, ½ gill olive oil in a deep pan, sprinkle the chicken with salt and pepper, put in the hot fat and turn frequently until slightly browned on all sides. Remove from the fire and drain off all superfluous fat and leave sufficient rich brown gravy to cover. Add ½ cup of thinly sliced mushrooms and a bay-leaf, cover the pot closely and place over a very moderate heat and simmer gently for 15 minutes. Arrange the chicken in pyramid form, pour the sauce over the chicken and surround with a border of riced potatoes.—*Mrs. J. Douglas Freeman, Baltimore.*

OLNEY INN

(OLNEY INN *grew from a small farm house that "served meals" to one of the most popular eating places in the Eastern countryside. Its success was quite simply assured by good Maryland food, properly cooked and appetizingly served. It has been the determination of the management that the patrons would leave contented as only a patron can after a thoroughly enjoyed repast. Upon observing the astounding progress made by this establishment there is definite proof that the gastronomic resources of the Maryland Free State are sufficient in themselves to crown honest effort with success to the delight of the tourist and financial satisfaction of the management.)*

CHICKEN LIVERS WITH PILAFF INDIENNE

8 to 12 chicken livers, 3 tablespoonsful of butter, ½ teaspoonful (scant) of salt, ½ teaspoonful of pepper, 1 cup of rich stock, 3 teaspoonsful of wine if desired. Carefully remove the gall bladders from the livers; wash, wipe dry and season with the salt and pepper. Melt the butter in a frying pan. In it dispose the livers side by side and let cook briskly about three minutes, then turn and let cook three minutes on the other side. Add the broth, which should have been seasoned with vegetables and herbs, and let simmer five or six minutes. Season with more salt and pepper if needed. Add the wine if to be used.

Pilaff: 2½ cups of stock, 1 cup of tomato purée, 1 cup of rice (blanched) ½ teaspoonful of salt, ½ cup of butter, 1 teaspoonful of curry powder. Cook the blanched rice in the stock and purée, stirring occasionally with a silver fork or by shaking the saucepan, until the liquid is absorbed. Add the butter, creamed and mixed with the curry powder, and let cook over hot water until tender. Dispose the rice in a wreath on a serving dish and inside of it pour the livers and sauce. Serve very hot.—*Mrs. Clara May Downey, Olney Inn, Montgomery County.*

SPANISH CHICKEN

Cut up young chicken and put on to boil with small quantity of water, skin side down, with salt, pepper, and celery; stew until tender. Then remove chicken and in this gravy put 1½ cups of cream, one tablespoonful curry powder, 4 tablespoons flour, yolks of four eggs, one tablespoon paprika, add parsley the last thing.—*Mrs. J. Douglas Freeman, Baltimore.*

PRICE HOUSE, CUMBERLAND

Residence of the Father and Grandfather of Emily Post

CHICKEN WITH NOODLES

(A MARYLANDER *by birth, a member of the smart world wherever she may be, and of late years an author, Emily Post needs no further introduction. Her books, "Etiquette" and "The Personality of a House," heralded from one end of the country to the other, have established for her an unassailable reputation as an authority on all matters of good taste and the finer discriminations of culture.*)

4 cups of chicken cut in pieces inch size, 3 cups of cream sauce, 1 package of medium cut noodles.

Directions: Cook the noodles. Drain and spread around the edge of a pyrex pie plate. Put pieces of butter on top. Put in broiler about ten minutes or until brown. Mix the chicken and cream sauce and pour this in the center of the plate.—*Emily Post, Author of "Etiquette," and "The Personality of a House," etc.*

PANNED CHICKEN

Select chicken about three and a half or four pounds, joint and wash. Place in roasting pan. Dredge with flour, sprinkle with salt and pepper and dot over with butter. (Be generous with the butter.) About half cover with water and cook in moderate oven, turning chicken in essence as it browns. Add more water if necessary and cook until tender. Make gravy of the essence, a little milk, salt and pepper and thicken with a little flour.— *Mrs. J. H. Windsor, Windsor Manor, Baltimore County.*

CHICKEN MARYLAND

Take half spring chicken and season, rub over with flour, then immerse in beaten eggs. Heat some clarified butter in a saucepan, fry the chicken in it very slowly to cook and attain a fine color, then finish cooking in a slack oven for ten minutes. Dress the chickens with cream sauce, and garnish the top with small corn fritters and slices of broiled bacon, decorate the legs with paper frills.—*Mr. H. N. Busick, Managing Director, Lord Baltimore Hotel, Baltimore.*

STEWED CHICKEN

Two hours before dinner, put on the fire a quart of water, a small onion chopped fine, pepper and salt and let it simmer. Cut up a chicken and lay it in fresh water. An hour before dinner put it in the broth that has been simmering. When about to be dished, stir in a tablespoon of butter rolled in flour, a teacup of cream, with parsley cut up in it.—*Mr. and Mrs. George R. Dennis, Mt. Hampton, Frederick County.*

BONED SQUAB CHICKEN WITH DRESSING

Take 1 pound squab chicken and thoroughly bone (excepting drum sticks). Stuff with dressing made from veal, ground fine, that has been mixed with white of egg and cream. Season dressing with salt, pepper and nutmeg, also cooked sherry. Place in oven until done, garnish and serve.—*Mr. H. B. Grimshaw, Baltimore Steam Packet Co., Baltimore.*

GIBLET HASH WITH POACHED EGG

Wash sufficient giblets to serve number desired. Place in cold salted water and boil until tender. Remove from liquid and cut into small pieces. Return to liquid, add potatoes diced, one carrot and one finely chopped onion, a sprig of celery diced, a few thyme leaves, salt and pepper to taste. When vegetables are cooked thicken the stew with a little flour. Serve on toast triangles and top with a poached egg for each portion.—*Mrs. J. H. Windsor, Windsor Manor, Baltimore County.*

ROAST GOOSE

Thoroughly clean and dry the bird, then stuff it with mashed potatoes, seasoned with onions, sage, salt and pepper, or equal parts of bread crumbs, chopped apples and boiled onions, seasoned with sage, salt and pepper.

Stew and truss. Put in a hot oven for three-quarters of an hour. When considerable oil has been extracted, pour it off. Dredge with flour and baste often. Garnish with water cress.—*D. Charles Winebrener, Frederick County.*

ROASTED GUINEA HEN

Make a savory stuffing from minced chicken, ham, onions, sage and bread crumbs, and stuff the Guinea with this. Place slices of fat salt pork over their breasts and roast in a covered pan, basting every ten minutes with chicken stock and melted butter. Serve with currant jelly.—*D. Charles Winebrener, Frederick County.*

DEVILED TURKEY LEGS

(*Chicken legs or ham may be substituted*)

Mix an even teaspoon of mustard in ½ cup of water, fill cup with milk or cream, add small lump of butter (about ½ tablespoonful). Put on in frying pan with turkey and let all warm together. About fifteen minutes is sufficient.—*John Ridgely, Hampton, Baltimore County.*

BONELESS TURKEY

1 turkey about 8 or 10 pounds, 5 pound leg of veal raw, 1 ham raw, around 8 pounds, use half inch lengthwise strips ½ inch by ½ inch in thickness and width, 2 cans mushrooms whole, 2 cans truffles, cut in pieces, 2 pounds western side, cut in strips, 1 quart chestnuts, boiled and shelled.

Split the turkey down the back and lay open on table, removing all bones and laying the meat back in place as near original as possible, being careful not to break the outer skin. Grind the meat from the leg of veal and line the entire inside of the turkey. Then lay a strip of ham, a row of mushrooms, a strip of western side, a row of chestnuts, a strip of ham, a row of truffles and repeat until all are used. Then cover with the rest of the veal. Roll turkey up carefully but firmly in a cloth and let boil gently for four hours.

Take the leg bone of the veal, a calf's head and a beef shin and boil until all jelly has been extracted. Season highly with salt, pepper and paprika. Have an oblong mold with high sides to fit the turkey. Line the mold with the jelly. Chill. When set, decorate with flowers and fancy objects made out of boiled beets, carrots, eggs, and parsley for foliage. Place turkey in mold, cover all with the jelly and chill thoroughly. Turn out on large platter and slice for serving. A beautiful and most delicious dish.— *Mr. Rudolph Kaiser, Anne Arundel County.*

TURKEY STUFFING

Boil and drain one pound of cut macaroni. Boil the gizzard and heart for an hour and a half, then put in the liver and boil for half an hour longer, cut these fine and mix with the macaroni. Season with chopped onion, poultry seasoning, salt and pepper. Do not fill the turkey too full of the stuffing, for it will swell in the roasting.—*D. Charles Winebrener, Frederick County.*

STUFFED ROAST SQUAB

Pluck and wash well. Make a dressing of bread crumbs. Season well with onion, butter, salt and pepper. With this fill the pockets of the squab. Put in roaster, two inches apart. Take the broth from pork or beef roast, mix with the chicken broth and pour over the stuffed squabs. Roast in slow oven. Baste frequently. Increase heat to brown the squabs. Serve each squab on an individual platter, with the brown gravy. Garnish with parsley and pimento cheese rings with crisp pickle.—*Miss Margaret Lentz Miller, Garrett County.*

TUDOR HALL, HARFORD COUNTY (See receipt, page 88)

PANNED CHICKENS

Prepare the chickens as for broiling. Take a few bread crumbs and mix them with parsley chopped fine, pepper and salt. *Half* broil the chickens, dip them in melted butter and then in bread crumbs and then pan them.—*Mr. and Mrs. George R. Dennis, Mt. Hampton, Frederick County.*

CURRY

Chicken or turkey raw or cold boiled cut up as for stew, take 2 tablespoonfuls of curry powder, one teaspoonful ginger, one teaspoonful salt, 3 tablespoonfuls flour, two yolks of hard boiled eggs, 2 pints of water, mash the eggs well, add the other ingredients, stir in the water gradually, add the meat and stew all up for a little while. Serve with boiled rice in a separate dish. *Mrs. Robert Goldsborough Henry, Myrtle Grove, Talbot County.*

BRAISED DUCKLING BIGARRADE

(TOURISTS *coming east on the scenic route 40 will be pleased to learn that a well cooked meal always awaits one at the Fort Cumberland Hotel in Cumberland, Maryland.*)

Put whole duckling in a saucepan with very little lard or butter. Add carrots, onions and celery; cook a little brown; and then sprinkle with a little flour and cook until the flour is well browned; add some tomato purée and cover the duckling with stock; cover the pan and put in a moderate oven until the duckling is well done. Then remove and add to the gravy a cupful of currant jelly; cook until jelly is well dissolved; put the juice of two oranges and juice of one lemon in and strain. Take the two oranges and lemon peel, cut very fine, about 1½ inches long, and boil until tender. Drain water off and add the peel to the gravy; serve with quartered orange.

Note: If the gravy is too thin, thicken it with cornstarch. This will make a very palatable dish for all year round.—*Mr. Ivan W. Poling, Manager, Fort Cumberland Hotel, Allegany County.*

EDWIN BOOTH AS "HAMLET"

"My father, Edwin Booth, was fond of Southern cooking and employed colored cooks by preference. I remember his speaking of the terrapin offered by his Baltimore hosts at dinner. He was especially fond of canvas back ducks, and once sent from London to Baltimore for some as a gift to an English friend. The receipts submitted are from Tudor Hall, Bel Air, Maryland, his birthplace."
—*Edwina Booth Crossman.*

ROAST TURKEY

Select a plump turkey and clean well. Make a stuffing of three cups of stale bread, crumbled fine and moistened. Add the liver and a slice of boiled ham, minced fine, a hash of onion and parsley, salt and pepper to taste. Mix well, adding if desired two well beaten eggs, and fill the turkey. Season the fowl with lard, salt and pepper. Put in roasting oven with small quantity of water, simply enough to prevent the pan from burning at the start. Baste frequently with essence from the pan. Roast, not too fast, until well done and a golden brown.—*Edwina Booth Crossman, daughter of Edwin Booth, from Tudor Hall, birthplace of Edwin Booth, Harford County.*

EGGS

POACHED EGGS WITH TOMATOES
AND MUSHROOMS

6 eggs, 3 large tomatoes, 1½ lbs. chopped mushrooms, 2 tablespoons butter, ½ tablespoon chopped parsley, ½ tablespoon flour, 1 cup bouillon or cream, salt and pepper.

Directions: Slice and fry the tomatoes. Boil the mushrooms in the bouillon or cream for a minute or so. Drain off and fry in butter. Stir in flour, parsley, salt and pepper. Pour bouillon over it. Poach the eggs. Put the slices of tomato on a platter. On some put the poached eggs and on the others the mushrooms.—*Emily Post, Author of "Etiquette," and "The Personality of a House," etc.*

EGGS À LA CRÊME

Boil 12 eggs just hard enough to allow you to cut them in slices. Put them in a moderately deep dish with alternate layers of grated bread, salt and pepper.

Sauce à la Crême

Put ¼ pound butter with a tablespoon of flour rubbed into it, in a saucepan, add some chopped parsley, a very little onion, salt, pepper, nutmeg to taste—but not too much—and a gill of cream or rich milk. Stir it over the fire until it begins to boil, then pour over the eggs, cover the top with grated bread and small lumps of butter. Put it in the oven and when a light brown, send it to the table.—*John Ridgely, Hampton, Baltimore County*

MARK TWAIN, *to grocer in small town in which he was to lecture that evening:*
"Is there anything for a stranger to do or to see in town this evening?"
"Not that I know of, sir. Although there's probably going to be a lecture some-
where tonight, I've been selling eggs all day."

EGG CROQUETTES

Put through meat chopper hard boiled eggs and parsley, add
salt, pepper, celery salt, and touch of onion. Add to this enough
cream sauce to make moist enough to mold. Roll croquettes in
eggs and crumbs, brown in deep fat.—*Miss Mary McDaniel,
Talbot County.*

BEVERLY

("BEVERLY," *in Worcester County, the ancestral home of the Dennises, is one of the most interesting of Maryland homesteads. While the residence was started as late as 1774, the original patent of the land dates back to 1669. The dignity and taste which pervade the old home form a quite natural background for a family which has contributed so liberally to their state and country leaders in the varied fields of statesmanship, jurisprudence, literature and finance.*)

EGGS IN ASPIC

Six hard boiled eggs, 2 cups beef aspic flavored with 1 tablespoon tarragon vinegar, Mayonnaise, 1 tablespoon cream.

Directions: Cut the eggs in two, remove yolks, and mix them with enough Mayonnaise and cream to make them smooth and creamy. Fill the whites of eggs with the mixture and join the halves together. Break the aspic with fork, make a nest of it and place the eggs in the center.—*Emily Post, Author of "Etiquette," and "The Personality of a House," etc.*

OMELETTE SOUFFLE

Take the whites of six eggs and beat them until they are hard, then take the yolks of two eggs with six tablespoonfuls of sugar and beat them together. Flavor it with any essence agreeable to your taste. When the above is well mixed then put the whole together and put it in a dish with a little butter rubbed on it and bake until the top is slightly brown. The oven must be hot on the bottom as well as on top.—*Mrs. Wm. H. Thomas, Carroll County.*

SCRAMBLED EGGS

4 tablespoons of milk, salt, pepper (after you take from fire) 6 eggs, butter the size of a walnut. Beat eggs all together, and 4 tablespoons of milk. Put butter in pan and when melted add eggs. Keep stirring for a few moments over fire until done.—*John Ridgely, Hampton, Baltimore County.*

MARYLAND OMELET

Two eggs, one quarter cup milk, one teaspoon cornstarch, one pinch salt, one pinch of black pepper. Beat the eggs light—add the cornstarch to the milk, mix together, add one teaspoon butter, one tablespoon of bacon fat, pour into pan. Cook until it sets and then put it in the oven for three minutes. This can be used with bacon or ham, anything at all, any portion that is left over can be warmed up for the next meal. Never falls.—*Mrs. James H. Preston, Baltimore.*

YOUNG ARTIST: *"Don't you think, sir, that this painting of mine is—er—tolerable?"*
WHISTLER: *"What is your opinion of a tolerable egg?"*

SPANISH OMELETTE

One 3 lb. can tomatoes, ½ oz. extract of beef (or beef juice), 1 sliced onion, 2 tablespoonsful olive oil, 1 sliced green pepper, ½ lb. mushrooms (or one can), salt and pepper to taste. Put the tomatoes, green peppers, extract of beef and olive oil in a stew pan and cook for two hours, then add the onions and mushrooms and cook for twenty minutes longer. Make an omelette of six eggs, fill and garnish with the foregoing ingredients.—*D. Charles Winebrener, Frederick County.*

MARSH HEN EGGS

A marsh hen is a migratory salt-water fowl indigenous to the salt marshes of the Eastern Shore of Maryland. I can remember thirty-five years ago when they used to be gathered in bushel baskets for family consumption. They were very thin shelled and likely to absorb the flavor of articles next to which they may have been placed. In cooking them it was only necessary to have fairly hot water—not boiling—in which they would cook as much as desirable in from two to three minutes.—*Chief Judge Samuel K. Dennis, of Baltimore City and Worcester County.*

EGGS, JOCKEY CLUB

Split English muffins, toast and spread lightly with butter; over each half muffin set a thin slice of boiled ham, carefully broiled; above the ham set an egg poached in water just below the boiling point; over the eggs pour cream sauce in which a few fresh mushrooms, split through the caps and stems, have been simmering. Serve immediately. One cup of sauce for three eggs.— *D. Charles Winebrener, Frederick County.*

SHIRRED EGGS

Take a shirred egg dish, brush it inside with melted butter, pour in two or three eggs as the case may be, set it in a moderate oven until the eggs are just set, then serve.—*Mr. H. R. Bowen, Chesapeake Steamship Company, Baltimore.*

EGGS WITH TOMATO AND RICE

(*3 persons*)

2 cups boiled rice, 1 cup tomato sauce, 3 eggs, 1 tablespoon bread crumbs, 2 tablespoons grated cheese.

Directions: Mix the rice and the tomato sauce, put in a baking dish. Put the whole, unbroken eggs on top. A layer of bread crumbs next and over this the grated cheese. Bake in a hot oven for about ten minutes.—*Emily Post, Author of "Etiquette," and "The Personality of a House," etc.*

MEATS

ROAST BEEF AND GRAVY

For six persons secure the second cut of a rib roast. Have the lower half of the ribs removed and the skirt sewed by the butcher to the large end of the roast. Sprinkle both sides with pepper and salt and place in a baking pan in an oven hot enough to sear the meat at once and prevent the juices from escaping. As soon as the meat is brown turn over and sear the other side. Then reduce the heat somewhat and cook one hour if the roast is to be rare, longer if well done. When cooked, pour most of the excess fat from the pan. Then take a heaping cooking spoonful of flour and smooth in a small bowl to a paste with a little water. When the lumps are out add cold water enough to make one pint. Remove the roast from the baking pan to a hot platter and place in the oven to keep hot. Transfer the baking pan to a flame on top of the stove and pour into the remaining fat the thickened flour and water, stirring briskly with the flat side of the spoon to prevent lumps until the gravy is of the desired consistency. Add salt and pepper and serve.—*Katherine Scarborough, Baltimore.*

BEEF TONGUE

Take a fresh beef tongue and boil until tender, in just enough water to cover it. When you boil the tongue put a few bay-leaves in and boil with it. This ought to give you about a pint of liquor. Add to this liquor one-half pint of California Port, one glass currant jelly with one piece of mace and salt to taste. Pour this mixture over the tongue after it has had skin removed and stew slowly for one hour, and serve hot.—*Mrs. Charles H. Tilghman, Gross' Coate, Talbot County.*

HAYFIELDS

("HAYFIELDS," *considered one of the most perfectly designed Manors of Mary-land, was completed by Col. Nicholas Merryman Bosley in 1808. It is replete with historic interest. In 1824 when the Marquis de Lafayette revisited the scenes of his former victories, he offered a lusty tankard of silver for the most perfectly developed Maryland farm. It was won by "Hayfields," presented to Col. Bosley and is still in the family from which the ownership of "Hayfields" has never passed. Later it was John Merryman in 1852 who imported to "Hay-fields" the first Hereford cattle to be brought to this country.*)

ROAST BEEF

The first thing to do to have good roast beef is to buy the best cuts. Only the first or second cut of the heaviest beef should be used and none should be purchased lighter than two ribs, which should run about eight or nine pounds. This should be a standing roast.

Wipe the meat carefully and powder with salt, pepper and a very little flour. Put about a half cup of water in the bottom of the roasting pan and place beef in it, standing. Never let it lie on its side. Baste every fifteen minutes for the first hour.

For rare beef allow one hour and twenty minutes for eight pounds. Five minutes for each additional pound, in a hot oven.

Around this beef put Irish potatoes. Turn these when basting and they will be a golden brown, served around roast on same dish.

Remember only the first five ribs on a steer are the choice ones.—*Mrs. Anne Merryman Carroll, Hayfields, Baltimore County.*

MINCE OF LAMB

One cup of gravy well thickened, the remains of cold roast lamb minced, but not very fine. Two tablespoonsful of cream, one salt spoonful of powdered mace, one small minced onion, pepper and salt to taste, one tablespoonful of butter, three eggs well whipped. Heat the gravy to a boil, add milk, butter, seasoning, onion and lastly the eggs—stir well and add the seasoned meat. Let it get smoking hot, but it must not boil. Serve on toast.
—*Mrs. Bartlett S. Johnston, Baltimore.*

ROULADE OF BEEF WITH MUSHROOMS

Take a piece of flank and trim all the fat off, and lay strips of bacon, one onion and one green pepper on the beef, roll it and tie it very tight with cord. Put it in the oven and roast it until it is nice and tender. Slice and serve with mushroom sauce on top.—*Dining Car Service, B. & O. R.R.*

BEEF KIDNEY STEW (*Very Fine*)

Soak kidneys an hour in cold salt water. Cut in small pieces, removing gristle. Put in skillet ⅛ lb. butter in which cook one chopped onion and three tablespoons flour to a golden brown, stirring constantly. To this add 2 quarts hot water. Put in cut up kidney and allow to simmer from early morn till evening, taking at least two hours to come to bubble. The next morning allow to boil, add seasoning and serve. It will need more water the first day as the gravy thickens.—*Mrs. Charles B. Trail, Frederick County.*

CORNING BEEF

To 4 gallons water, 6 pounds salt, 2 ounces saltpetre, 1½ pounds brown sugar. Salt beef and let lay in a cool place 4 or 5 days. Then pack in a close barrel and pour the above mixture upon it. The drying pieces are ready for use in 3 weeks—the other in a month.—*Mrs. Sarah D. Avirett Thomas, Allegany County.*

COWPUNCHER: *"Hey, Waiter, take this steak out and have it cooked."*
WAITER: *" 'Tis cooked."*
COWPUNCHER: *"Cooked, hell, I've seen cows hurt worse than that and get well."*

TO COOK A BEEFSTEAK

The steak should be fully 1½ inches in thickness. Wash it and dry it with a towel. Put it on a clear good fire to broil. Have a dish heated and when one side of the steak is partly done, take it from the fire and put it on the warm dish and press it with a knife blade *very gently* that the juice may flow into the dish but do not bruise the steak. Then return it to the fire the raw side down and when that is partly done remove it again to the dish and press it as before. Then return it to the fire (keeping the gravy warm) and broil it until done. Then lay it on the dish of warm gravy, add to it a piece of butter the size of a shellbark (or walnut) and season the steak with black pepper and salt. It takes about ten minutes to cook and should never be seasoned until done.—*Mrs. Charles H. Tilghman, Gross' Coate, Talbot County.*

BRUNSWICK STEW

1 chicken cut into small pieces, 1 cup fresh corn, 1 cup potatoes blocked (raw), 1 cup fresh lima beans, ½ cup tomato juice, 4 slices of bacon cut into small pieces, 2 tablespoons thickening. Cook the chicken, add vegetables, cut up bacon and add to the mixture last. Salt and pepper to taste.—*Mrs. Joseph C. Byron, Washington County.*

BAKED CALF'S HEAD

One calf's head—have butcher remove eyes and clean thoroughly. Allow it to stand in cold water for an hour to draw the blood. Then take it out, wash thoroughly, put in a pot of cold water and allow it to cook until the meat drops from the bone. Then chop fine every part, including the tongue, brain, etc., moisten the chopped meat with the liquor in which it was cooked and add ½ teaspoon whole cloves, a few allspice, ½ cupful of cooking sherry and put in a baking dish with a few bread crumbs on top, just enough to brown, and put in oven long enough to heat through, or until the crumbs are brown. Serve with slices of lemon.—*Mrs. Samuel T. Earle, Baltimore.*

PAN RAREBIT

3 Faces (or other pieces of pork not used for sausage), 3 livers, 2 lbs. beef (round), salt, pepper, sage, cornmeal (about two lbs.). Boil in water sufficient to cover them until meat leaves the bones. Then pick and grind as for sausage. Then put back into water meat was boiled in, about 1 gal., add pepper, salt, sage to taste and cornmeal, making mixture about the consistency of mush. Boil altogether. Then put in pans or dishes. When needed cut into slices and heat in frying pan until brown. (This is a delicious breakfast dish.)—*Mrs. Frank S. Hambleton, Baltimore County.*

LAMB CHOP BRASSEUR

Cut lamb chops (thick) from the end of a loin. Trim to a neat appearance. Season with cayenne pepper and salt. Butter lightly on both sides and broil on a hot charcoal fire. Serve on a hot dish and pour over the chops a gravy of butter. Season well with salt and pepper and the juice of a lemon.—*Edwina Booth Crossman, daughter of Edwin Booth, from Tudor Hall, birthplace of Edwin Booth, Harford County.*

FRIED LIVER

Cut the liver in *thin* slices, season with pepper and salt, fry quickly otherwise it will be hard and dry. After taking the meat out of the pan, add to the juice that is left a piece of butter rolled in flour to make the gravy.—*Mr. and Mrs. George R. Dennis, of Mt. Hampton, Frederick County.*

HAMPTON

("HAMPTON," started in 1783 by Captain Charles Ridgely and finished in 1790, is one of the stateliest and most pretentiously dignified of all Maryland manors. From its cupola, commanding a view of Baltimore County for miles around, to the wistaria festooned portico, it bespeaks the aristocracy which heritage has bestowed so lavishly upon it. Within, the great hall of impressive dimensions (60 feet by 32 feet) divides the first floor, the dining room and sitting room on one side, and the music room and drawing room on the other. The massive furniture, stained glass windows and the magnificent portrait of Miss Eliza Ridgely by Sully contribute an old world aura that will long linger in one's memory. The ground, originally five thousand acres, is meticulously maintained, its boxwood gardens being well worth a trip to see, while the family vault in the middle of the ancestral burial ground, surrounded by a high brick wall and at the end of a lane of large and somber cedar and yew trees, must have proven a treat in the moonlight to Edgar Allan Poe, were he ever so fortunate as to have seen it.)

CALF'S HEAD—WHOLE

(Receipt of Susan Harris, colored cook, 1880)

Wash first, then put to soak in cold water well sprinkled with salt, 1 hour. Take out brains and parboil. Put on in cold water and allow to boil slowly for 2 hours or until the flesh is very tender. Extract bones and draw skin off of tongue. Sprinkle inside with handful of salt—shake on black pepper; stick through it about 10 or 12 cloves and squeeze lemon juice over it. Then turn head over carefully folding it together and carry out same process on that side. Put away till time to bake in oven.

Beat up egg. Put it with bread crumbs over head. Steam about 1 tablespoonful of sage, thyme, strain over head and baste with it till it is browned and take it out of hot oven and keep hot till time to serve. Brains to be covered with egg and browned in pan with a little butter, and serve on dish with head.—*John Ridgely, Hampton, Baltimore County.*

HOG'S HEAD CHEESE

Remove the skins from the head and feet (only fore-feet are used), and use the tongues from the youngest and best hogs. Boil them till quite tender and easily stripped off the bones. Chop small and season with salt and pepper to taste. Some beaten cloves, sage and sweet marjoram, mix well together with the hand. Press and eat it with vinegar and mustard.—*Mrs. Robert Goldsborough Henry, Myrtle Grove, Talbot County.*

PIG'S FEET, CHAFING DISH

Take six large pig's feet cooked but not pickled, free from all bone. Cut in small pieces, then put in chafing dish and season highly with salt, pepper, butter and a wine glass of Sherry wine. Cook about half an hour or until the seasoning strikes through well. *Serve very hot.—Mrs. J. Douglas Freeman, Baltimore.*

MATTAPANY

("Mattapany" *was granted to Henry Sewell in 1663. His widow Jane married Governor Charles Calvert, who subsequently became Lord Baltimore (from whom Miss Louisa Ogle Thomas is the tenth in descent). He erected the present building in 1674. Until quite recently the estate has been in possession of the Calvert family and their descendants and has been in the Thomas family for four generations.*)

PLATTER DINNER

Boil about eight small potatoes in their jackets. Pare and boil a bunch of carrots and cut in quarters lengthwise. Take sirloin steak about two inches thick and pepper and salt to taste, place in baking dish, cover with chopped onions, green pepper and diced celery and pour over it a bottle of catsup, or if preferred, tomato pulp. Dot with butter. Add cup of water, after it bakes one-half hour add the pared potatoes and carrots and bake until meat is tender. When ready to serve, carefully place steak on dish with carrots and potatoes around it and pour gravy over.—*Mrs. Ida Kenney, Baltimore.*

MEAT SOUFFLE

Two cups of ground meat, two tablespoons butter, three eggs, two cups of milk, two tablespoons of flour. Melt butter, add flour, milk and meat and eggs last. Bake thirty minutes.—*Miss Louisa Ogle Thomas, Mattapany, St. Mary's County.*

CREAMED CALVES' BRAINS

Blanch brains by parboiling. Remove all bits of skin. Cool brains by placing in bowl of cold water. Cut in pieces about one inch square.

Cook together, one tablespoonful flour, one tablespoonful of butter and one cup of rich milk. Add salt-spoonful of salt and pepper to taste.

When sauce is perfectly smooth and thick add tablespoonful minced parsley and the brains. Stir until well heated, then add well beaten yolk of one egg, stirring for one minute without boiling. Garnish a small dish with little triangles of toast and pour over them the creamed brains. If desired a half wine glass of sherry may be added.—*Mrs. Ida Kenney, Baltimore.*

PORK CHOPS

On each chop place a tomato, one tablespoon rice, slice of onion, strip green pepper and around it put chopped celery. Brown chop first and put each layer on and bake three hours in slow oven. Chop should be cut one inch thick.—*Miss Mary Mc-Daniel, Talbot County.*

SWEETBREADS

One medium sized pair of sweetbreads. Sauce: One half cup mushrooms, two tablespoons butter, two tablespoons flour, one half teaspoonful salt, a little white pepper and cayenne, one cup cream.

Soak sweetbreads in cold water thirty minutes. Drain and plunge into boiling water to which has been added a tablespoonful of lemon juice or vinegar, a bit of parsley and celery. Simmer fifteen minutes and add salt before done. Drain and put in cold water, and remove tough parts and skin. Then put in sauce.— *Miss Louisa Ogle Thomas, Baltimore.*

COLONIAL MARYLAND SAUSAGE

To fifty pounds of lean and fat fresh pork (three to four parts lean to one part fat) mix twelve ounces of table salt, one and one-half ounces of powdered saltpetre, four ounces of ground black pepper and red (podcayenne) one-half ounce.

Mix thoroughly and grind, not too fine or it will shrink too much after being cooked.

When ground or chopped properly, mix again with hands or paddle. Then stuff into casings previously cleansed inside and out.

Smoke the same with hickory wood and you will have the best country sausage dish ever placed before you, provided buckwheat cakes accompany them smoking hot.—*Miss Lilian Schley, Cousin of Admiral Winfield Scott Schley, Hero of the Spanish-American War, Frederick County. (This receipt is said to date back to 1740.)*

MARTINGHAM

("MARTINGHAM," *Talbot County, near St. Mary's, was completed in 1677 and was the original manor of William Hambleton.*)

TO STEW MUTTON CHOPS

Take 2 or 3 tablespoonsful of tomatoes according to the size of the dish, put it in a stew pan. Fry an onion and put with it, season the chops and put them in the pan with the tomatoes, a large piece of butter, a little water and let it cook one-half hour. —*Mrs. Charles H. Tilghman, Gross' Coate, Talbot County.*

SAUSAGE MEAT

To 20 pounds sausage meat put 6 ounces salt, 4 ounces ground black pepper and 1 teacup sage.—*Mrs. Mittie Plummer Bowling, Prince George County.*

MOCK TERRAPIN IN CHAFING DISH

Take one calf's liver, have butcher remove the gall, cut the liver in pieces about the size of the palm of your hand, boil until tender, take it out, and lay it on a dish to cool, then remove skin and cut it in small pieces. Take 6 eggs and hard boil, then mash the yolks in the liquor that is in the dish where the liver was laid. Put liver in the chafing dish, add yolks to the liver, season with red pepper and salt, put slices of butter over the liver. Put top on the chafing dish, and light lamp under it, keep top on while cooking. Add one wine-glass of sherry and mix well, put top back, and let it stand five minutes, and serve.—*Mrs. Bernard Freeman, Baltimore.*

COUNTRY SAUSAGE

Have meat cut up in even sized strips and squares, then weigh accurately:—Eight pounds of fat, twelve pounds of lean, spread out and season before grinding with one tablespoon of black pepper, two tablespoonsful of red pepper, three tablespoonsful of sage. One small teacup of salt for twenty pounds meat which has been thoroughly ground fine and worked well after grinding to make even mass. Stuff in casings before becoming cold.—*Mr. and Mrs. J. Spence Howard, St. Mary's Manor, St. Mary's County.*

SAUSAGE

30 pounds meat, 6 ounces salt, 1½ ounces black pepper, ¾ ounces red pepper and 4 ounces sage.—*General Francis E. Waters, Baltimore.*

SAUSAGE

(ON *the crest of a high hill overlooking the famous Green Spring Valley is Wickcliffe, the residence and estate of Dr. and Mrs. Walter Forman Wickes. While the residence is of comparatively recent structure, culinary traditions of the past are strictly observed, and the old receipt books which served the family for generations past in Kent County, and from which these receipts have been culled are still in active service.*)

To be made entirely of pork.

Seven pounds lean to be cut from underneath the shoulder, three pounds fat to be cut from the backbone, three-quarter cup of ground and sifted sage, one and one-half ounces of ground pepper, three ounces of salt.

If the sausage is cased, smoke it altogether three or four days by hanging up kitchen chimney or in a smoke house until the skin looks dry and dark. Then hang it up in the garret or any dry place.—*Dr. Walter Forman Wickes, Wickcliffe, Greenspring Valley, Baltimore County.*

SAUSAGE

2 cups sage, 1 cup pepper, 1½ cups salt. Mix thoroughly. Sprinkle over 45 pounds of meat cut in small pieces. Work seasoning in thoroughly. Grind twice.—*John B. Gray, Calvert County.*

SAUSAGE

To every 10 pounds of pork meat (tenderloin), mix 1 ounce sage, 2 ounces pepper, 3 ounces salt. Cut meat in small pieces, put in seasoning, then grind fine.—*Miss Mary W. Crisfield, Somerset County.*

129

"Auntie, you know how to make hash, don't you?"
"How do you make hash?! Don't you know, nobody makes hash; hash just naturally accumulates!"

SCRAPPLE

One jowl and one liver. Boil until it is well done, take out all the bones, run the meat through sausage cutter, then throw it in the water it was boiled in, season with salt, pepper, sage, thicken with cornmeal the consistency of thin mush; put in pans and slice off to fry.—*Mrs. J. Morsell Roberts, Calvert County.*

WOODMONT CLUB FAMOUS SAUSAGE

Use the hams of the hog with the other parts in making the sausage. Season with salt and pepper but do not put any sage or spices in as this ruins the flavor of the sausage. Always stuff in casings, as it does not absorb so much grease when cooking.—*Woodmont Rod and Gun Club, Woodmont, Washington County.*

RAGOUT SWEETBREADS—CHAMILLON

Make a rich gravy of knuckle of veal, seasoned with pepper, salt, cinnamon, and cloves pounded. It is greatly improved by adding a little of the stock from calves feet, before it is seasoned; it stiffens it. Parboil the sweetbreads and put them in the gravy and let them stew until done. Constantly baste while cooking until they acquire a pretty brown color. Put into the gravy about 15 drops of pure lemon juice. One knuckle of veal is enough for 8 sweetbreads. Also one clove and a piece of flat cinnamon one inch long will be sufficient for 4 sweetbreads.—*Mrs. Charles H. Tilghman, Gross' Coate, Talbot County.*

SWISS STEAK

2 lbs. round or flank steak, ½ cup flour, 3 tablespoonsful drippings or fat, 1 tablespoon green pepper, 1 small can tomatoes, 1 medium size union, 1 cup water, ¼ teaspoon black pepper, salt, dash Worcestershire sauce.

Wash steak and pat to absorb most of moisture. Sift flour over steak, patting into the steak as much as you can. Put drippings into frying pan and let get very hot, then put steak in and let it brown on both sides. When browned remove steak to roasting pan in which you have put some drippings. Put the cup of water into frying pan and let come to boil, stirring to remove browned flour from the bottom of pan. Next pour this boiling water over steak, add onion chopped fine, tomatoes, chopped green pepper, salt, black pepper and Worcestershire. Cover roasting pan and bake in slow oven two hours.—*Mrs. J. H. Windsor, Windsor Manor, Baltimore County.*

JELLIED TONGUE

One boiled tongue, two ounces gelatine dissolved in one-half pint cold water. One teacup browned gravy, one pint of liquor in which tongue was boiled, one tablespoonful sugar, three tablespoonsful vinegar, one pint boiling water. Cut tongue in slices, let jelly cool and begin to thicken. Wet mold in cold water, put in a little jelly, then tongue and so on, until mold is filled. Set in a cool place. Other meat is also good when prepared in this way.—*Mrs. Dawson Orme George, Caroline County.*

VEAL CROQUETTES

Chop cold veal and sweetbreads very fine, season with pepper, salt, nutmeg and melted butter. Beat up an egg, flour your hands, and form meat into balls. Fry like crullers. Decorate with parsley.—*Dr. Walter Forman Wickes, Wickcliffe, Greenspring Valley, Baltimore County.*

VEAL PATÉ (JELLY)

1 lb. veal, 4 hard boiled eggs (sliced), 1 tablespoonful gelatine. Boil veal in small quantity of water until tender. Cut very fine and season to taste with salt, celery seed and pepper. Fill a buttered mold with alternate layers of the veal and the eggs, add gelatine to the water in which the veal was cooked and let it boil a few minutes. When this is cool (not cold) pour it over the mold of the veal and eggs and place in a cool place. Serve cold.—*Miss Clara Hollyday, Readbourne, Queen Anne's County.*

PRESSED VEAL OR CHICKEN WITH EGG

Boil any quantity of veal until tender, chop. Line a mold with sliced hard boiled eggs. Season liquor with salt and pepper; a dash of other spice is sometimes tasty. Add the veal and arrange in mold. Whole boiled eggs may also be buried in the chopped meat. The meat need not be solidly pressed. Enough liquor may be prepared and gelatine added to fill in spaces with the meat jelly.—*Mrs. Dawson Orme George, Caroline County.*

YORKSHIRE PUDDING

Take 3 eggs; 1 pt. of milk; 6 large tablespoonfuls of flour; ½ teaspoon salt; 2 dashes of pepper. Beat the eggs, whites and yolks together, until light and add to them the milk. Put flour in bowl and mix gradually with the eggs and milk. Strain through a fine sieve. Add salt and pepper and bake. (I understand that the original custom was to bake it under the beef, but at home the pudding was poured into the dripping pan after the beef had been roasted.)—*Mrs. T. Edward Hambleton, Baltimore County.*

THE COOKING AND STUFFING OF
HAMS AND THE CURING OF MEATS

After the Fashion of Old Maryland Manors

BAKED HAM

Soak for 48 hours (2 days) changing water after first 24 hours. Simmer quietly until done (until bone in hock is loosened and can be twisted or loosened from meat). Allow ham to cool in water in which it was boiled. Bake carefully in not too hot oven, after skinning and covering ham with brown sugar and sticking with cloves. Baste often.—*Mrs. Clara May Downey, Olney Inn, Montgomery County.*

HAM CROQUETTES

Take ¼ pound of cooked ham; beat the ham thoroughly in a mortar with a little of the fat, a small piece of butter and the yolks of two hard-boiled eggs. Add a tablespoon of well-boiled rice and a sprinkle of pepper, salt and cayenne. Mix all well together. Flour a board and divide the mixture into croquettes, three inches long and shaped like small sausages and roll in flour till smooth. Dip each one in a beaten egg and bread crumbs and fry in boiling lard. Serve on slices of hot buttered toast and garnish with rings of hard-boiled eggs and parsley.—*Mrs. Caroline A. Tyler, Baltimore (Courtesy of Mrs. Samuel T. Earle).*

TO COOK HAM

Cover with cold water and cook slowly, fifteen minutes to a pound. Let cool in the water, remove the skin and bake with essence, one teacup of sherry wine or vinegar and ½ cup of brown sugar.—*Mrs. G. H. Lilburn, Baltimore.*

BAKED HAM

Soak the ham in skimmed milk overnight. In the morning wash hard with coarse cloth or stiff brush, removing all mold or smoke from the outside. Put into a pot of cold water and allow to boil hard until the meat leaves the end bone. Skin off rind while the ham is hot then put in the oven and allow part of fat to stew down. Then allow to cool, cover with brown sugar and fill the remaining fat with cloves. Bake until brown, baste meanwhile with three cups of sherry, madeira or champagne.—*Frederic Arnold Kummer, Baltimore.*

TO CURE HAMS

To 500 pounds of meat, one peck of fine salt rubbed well into all parts of ham, especially the skin, using up the salt on that quantity of meat. Lay in a tight box with skin side down, one ham on the other, *for three or four days,* depending upon temperature. Remove from box on table, keeping all salt that has not been absorbed. To every ham allow ½ pound of brown sugar, ½ teaspoonful black pepper, ½ teaspoonful of saltpeter ground fine. Into the hock rub some fine red pepper and around the under joints. Rub the mixture of sugar, pepper, and saltpeter *well* into the hams, packing back the salt that was not dissolved. Put back in box skin down, let stay for six weeks, hang up, smoke with *hickory* wood—gentle smoke, sunshiny days—six times for five or six hours each time. Bag, dip each bag in a mediumly thin whitewash, hang up—ready for use in about five or six months.—*Mrs. John G. H. Lilburn, Baltimore.*

DIRECTIONS FOR COOKING OLD HAMS

Soak the ham overnight, wash or scrub well before putting it on to boil in COLD water, which should cover it. Let it boil SLOWLY until the bone in the end loosens. Remove the skin and put the ham back in the liquor until cold. Cover with a paste made of brown sugar and vinegar, then put in a very hot oven for fifteen or twenty minutes, or until nicely browned. Slice very thin.—*D. Charles Winebrener, Frederick County.*

TO CURE MT. HAMPTON HAMS

("MT. HAMPTON," *the residence of Mr. and Mrs. George R. Dennis, according to the original date on the house, was built in 1776. It was originally patented under the name of "Fat Oxen" but the name was changed in 1800 to Mt. Hampton. It has been in the Dennis family since 1820.*)

Rub each ham on the fleshy side with a teaspoonful of salt-peter and a large tablespoon of brown sugar and a dust of pepper. Then rub skin well with salt and *plenty in the hock,* now pack them well in a box skin side down, covering the bottom with salt before packing and sprinkling between layers.

At the end of six weeks, take out of box, rub well with borax, *forcing about a thimble full in the hock* as there is where the fly is apt to begin.

Hang up and smoke from three to five days, airing the smokehouse a little each day to prevent the meat getting warm while smoking.

Do the shoulders as you do the bones. Use hickory wood or apple wood for smoking.—*Mr. and Mrs. George R. Dennis, Mt. Hampton, Frederick County.*

TO CURE HAMS

Have meat thoroughly cold and keep out of sun while handling. As soon as cut up, rub with salt for 10 minutes, using as much salt as meat will absorb. Let lay in meat house three hours. Then use following mixture and rub each ham thoroughly twenty minutes.

Amounts for six hams:—

Two and one-half pounds of brown sugar, two and a half ounces saltpeter, ten ounces of black pepper. It will take about a peck of salt for eighteen hams, and after rubbing thoroughly as above, pack in sugar barrel skin side down for six weeks. Remove and hang up and smoke about six times, then seal up in cloth sacks and make air tight by dipping in lime.—*Mr. and Mrs. J. Spence Howard, St. Mary's Manor, St. Mary's County.*

CURING MEAT

3 pecks of fine salt, 3½ pounds of saltpeter (ground or beat very fine), 2 quarts of molasses, 4 teacups of ground black pepper, to every one thousand (1,000) pounds of pork. Mix well and rub meat.—*Mr. Henry Waring Clagett, Prince George County.*

TO CURE MEAT

To every thousand pounds of meat put three pecks of salt (one-half coarse), five pounds of saltpeter and some red pepper. Rub the skin side of the meat well with the hand.—*Miss Louisa Ogle Thomas, St. Mary's County.*

CHERRYFIELDS MANOR

("CHERRYFIELDS MANOR," *a fine old Colonial home originally built in 1777, burned down and rebuilt by William Coad in 1836, is now owned by Mr. J. F. Coad.*)

CURING PORK

To one hundred pounds, seven pounds coarse salt, five pounds brown sugar, two ounces saltpeter, one-half pound soda, four gallons of water. Rub meat on all sides with pepper and allow it to remain in brine for seven weeks.—*Mr. J. F. Coad, A.M., Cherryfields Manor, St. Mary's County.*

MEAT CURING PICKLE

(to 100 lbs. meat)

9 lbs. salt, 2½ lbs. brown sugar, 3 gal. water, ½ lb. black pepper, 2 oz. pearl ash. Dissolve well before using. Keep in pickle for 5 weeks. Hang up until dry, then smoke it with green hickory wood until the desired color and flavor are obtained.—*Mrs. Frank S. Hambleton, Baltimore County.*

CURING HAMS

½ bushel of salt, 2½ teacups saltpeter, 1 teacup red pepper, 2 teacups black pepper, 3 cups brown sugar. Mix thoroughly and rub on pork, when not frozen, next day after killing. Lay hams in bulk on shelf for six weeks or longer. Then hang up and smoke, using sassafras wood, if possible, for the fire—smoking until light brown. Then bag, dipping the bagged ham in lime or whitewash solution. Hang up until ready to use. Hams are better if not used for one year. Receipt cures about 20 hams weighing 10 or 12 pounds.—*John B. Gray, Calvert County.*

RECEIPT FOR CURING PORK

For each hundred pounds of meat (hams, shoulders, and sides), use one gallon New Orleans molasses, ¼ pound saltpeter, one string of red peppers and two pounds of brown sugar, add these ingredients to about two and a half gallons of water, and *boil* for about one-half an hour; keep stirring during the boiling process. When the boiling is finished place the pot in which the boiling was done in a cool place and let it become thoroughly cold.

Then make a brine of about eight or nine gallons of water with sufficient salt to float an egg, and add the boiled material to this brine.

Pack the meat in a water-tight container, preferably a barrel or barrels, *weighting* the same down so it cannot rise. Then pour the above mixture over the meat until it is thoroughly covered. Let stand for three or four weeks, depending upon the size of the hams and shoulders. At the end of which time remove meat from brine, wipe perfectly dry, hang up and smoke with either hickory or sassafras wood. Let the wood smoke but not blaze.

Before the meat is put in brine, it should be sprinkled with salt and allowed to stand overnight, so the blood will be drawn out, then wipe each piece with a damp cloth and then place in brine.—*Mrs. Charles Sterett Grason, Cornwalys Cross Manor, St. Mary's County.*

STUFFED HAM

Use 15 or 16 lb. ham, soak overnight in cold water. Next morning put fresh cold water on ham and let it come to a slow boil, and boil for 1 hour. Take one peck of spinach and one peck of kale, wash it thoroughly, remove all stems and chop very fine. Take a handful of the tops of shallots (a species of onion), chop it fine, add one teaspoonful of celery seed, salt and pepper to taste, mix all together. After ham has boiled an hour, remove it from water, and leave skin on. Take a long bread knife and make incisions or slits in the ham, as deep and as many as you can get in it. Dampen the stuffing (the greens and the seasoning) with the liquor the ham was boiled in and fill the incisions as full as you can. What is left over spread thick all over the top of the ham, and sew the ham in a large piece of cheesecloth covering, very tight, then put it back in the pot and boil slowly, allowing 15 minutes to each pound. When it is done, take it out of the water and leave the covering on until next morning, so that the ham will be thoroughly cold.—*Colonel John Douglas Freeman, Charles and St. Mary's Counties.*

143

GLASGOW

(THE *oldest portion of "Glasgow," Dorchester County, was built in 1760 by William Murray, the grandfather of William Vans Murray, who was Minister to the Netherlands 1797 to 1801. Later, in 1830, it came into the possession of Dr. Robert F. Tubman and has remained in the Tubman family ever since. It is interesting to learn that Mr. Robert E. Tubman was born in the massive four-poster in which he sleeps. His father was born and died in the same bed and his grandfather died in it. It is in a perfect state of preservation as is the entire mansion (which has been enlarged) and its contents. The receipts from "Glasgow" have been used by the Tubman family for generations.*)

SMITHFIELD HAM

Weigh the ham to be cooked and cover with cold water. Add handful of bay-leaves, let soak overnight. Next morning pour off water, add cold water to cover, and let come to a boil. Cook slowly, allowing fifteen minutes to the pound. Let stand in water it was cooked in until three-fourths cold. Put the ham in roasting pan, skin and sear both ways, stick with whole cloves, then make a dressing of: ½ pound brown sugar, ½ pint of vinegar, one dessert spoonful of mustard and half a teaspoonful of red pepper; cover the ham with this dressing, pour over one pint sherry wine, or cider, add two cups of pot liquor. Bake in quick oven for ½ hour, basting every five minutes.—*Mrs. Robert E. Tubman, Glasgow, Dorchester County.*

STUFFED HAM

This method of cooking hams originated with the early settlers of Maryland. After the fast of Lent it was considered imprudent to eat too greatly of fat meats and this method came into usage and it is yet used by many families at Eastertide.

1 peck of spinach, ¼ peck of chives, ¼ peck parsley. If the ham is an old one soak it in cold water for twelve hours. Wash carefully the spinach, chives and parsley, chop them fine by hand. Season with black and red pepper and salt. Make holes lengthwise in the ham with a steel. Push the ingredients into a hole until it is filled, then another hole until filled, until all ingredients have been used. Try to keep the holes separate so the filling will look round all through. Sew the ham in a piece of strong linen and boil twenty minutes to the pound—not longer. Let it cool in the liquor in which it is cooked and be perfectly cool before cutting.—*D. Charles Winebrener, Frederick County.*

TO CURE PORK

The bottom of the box should be sprinkled with salt before putting any of the meat into it. Rub well each ham and shoulder, back and front, with fine salt, then put about a teaspoonful of pulverized saltpeter on each ham and shoulder, rubbing it in well on the fleshy side and in the hock. Then sprinkle well with cayenne and black pepper, putting a big pinch of each in the hock. Cover the fleshy side with a liberal layer of brown sugar and about one-quarter of an inch of fine salt. Pack in an open box, so that the brine will run off, putting the hams in first, pack the shoulders upon the hams, cover each with a layer of fine salt. On top of the shoulders lay the middlings, salting each layer slightly.

Let the meat remain in salt for six weeks, then smoke for three weeks with green hickory wood, throwing in occasionally a few stalks of tobacco.

The hams should be kept a year before using.—*D. Charles Winebrener, Frederick County.*

HAM AND PINEAPPLE

(KATHERINE SCARBOROUGH'S *book, "Homes of the Cavaliers," dealing with the ancestral homes of Maryland's first families, stamps her as a most charming authority on her topic. Her volume, literally a "Blue Book" of Maryland Manors, tells of their history and traditions in the same gracious air as that which once permeated the very manors themselves.*)

Secure a slice, one inch thick, from the middle of a cured ham. Soak half a day in milk, or warm water will do. When ready to cook remove from the milk (if water is used the ham must be wiped off; otherwise not) and place in a hot pan with a piece of butter the size of a small egg. Cook slowly over the flame until brown. Then turn and brown the other side. Remove to another pan and place in a warm oven where it will keep hot but not cook. Have ready a can of sliced pineapple from which the juice has been drained off. Put the slices in the pan with the ham juice and brown on both sides. When this is done remove the ham from the oven to the platter upon which it is to be served and garnish with the cooked pineapple. Pour the ham and pineapple sauce over all.—*Katherine Scarborough, Baltimore.*

"I bought three hams here a month ago. Have you any more of them?"
"Yes, ma'am, there are ten hanging up there now."
"Well, if you're sure they're off the same pig I'll take two."

STUFFED HAM

Hams of twelve pounds or more are best to use for "stuffed ham," a popular dish with Southern Marylanders, particularly at Easter. The ham to be used is best when less than a year old.

For a sixteen-pound ham use one peck of greens: cabbage sprouts, turnip greens or kale, two dozen bunches of spring onions or their equivalent in chives, red and black pepper and celery seed.

Allow fifteen minutes per pound *after* the ham starts boiling and cook steadily until three-fourths done. Then put aside to partly cool while the greens scald in the ham liquor. When well wilted, take greens up and chop well. Season greens with celery seed and pepper to taste.

Then with a *sharp* knife cut crescent-shaped openings in the ham, top and bottom, as deep as the knife will go. Stuff the mixture of greens in the incisions, as much as they will hold. Make as many incisions as the ham will conveniently take.

Fold in a stout cloth and sew fast. Replace ham in the boiling liquor for the remaining quarter of the time allowed for cooking. Cool in the liquor, and when thoroughly cold, it is ready for use. Keep cloth on the ham to preserve the moisture and keep in a cool place. It is truly a dish for the gods.—*Mr. J. F. Coad, A.M., Cherryfields Manor, St. Mary's County.*

RECEIPT FOR CURING PORK AND BEEF

To every 100 pounds of pork, take four gallons water, eight pounds fine salt, two ounces good saltpeter, one and one-half ounce pearlash; two pounds broken sugar, or one quart molasses, made into a brine; when the meat is cool pack it into a tight vessel and pour the brine over it until corned. Let it remain under the brine about four to six weeks according to size. Take it out, rinse it in cold water, hang it up to dry and then smoke it some ten days or two weeks; during the month of March bag it and let it hang until used—from the sun.

Beef—put in brine, made after the same receipt, taking seven pounds of salt instead of eight. This receipt is invaluable—*Mrs. J. Alexis Shriver, Olney, Harford County.*

VEGETABLES

ARTICHOKES FROM ARMENIA

(GERALD W. JOHNSON *is well known in the literary world as a biographer and a novelist. His biographies, "Andrew Jackson" and "Randolph of Roanoke," have been among the most deservedly popular of the day. At present he is editorial writer on the staff of the Baltimore "Evening Sun.")*

Prepare the artichokes by cutting the spike from each leaf and cutting the top off flat, about half an inch from the end. Place them in plain boiling water for about ten minutes while preparing the second cooking water. Into this put the following, using these proportions for two artichokes and increasing if more are being cooked: one medium onion, cut in slices crosswise, two potatoes cut as for French frying, two lemons sliced crosswise, enough olive oil to cover the top of the vessel as it floats, and a goodly quantity of salt and pepper. After the artichokes have parboiled in the first water drain them off and put them in this second water which is either boiling or very near it. When they are tender remove them from the cooking water, setting them stem up in a bowl, with a slice of the cooked lemon on each stem. Remove the onions and potatoes and place in a separate bowl to cool. Serve the artichoke on lettuce, garnished with the onion and potatoes and plenty of mayonnaise.—*Gerald W. Johnson, Baltimore.*

STEWED CHESTNUTS

Remove the outer shells, then scald them to get the inner skin off and stew them in milk with a little salt until thoroughly cooked, but not broken to pieces. Then pour off the milk and thicken with a little flour and butter to make the white sauce. Put the sauce over the chestnuts and serve hot.—*Mrs. Bartlett S. Johnston, Baltimore.*

MYRTLE GROVE

(BECAUSE *over two hundred years ago the cavaliers of Maryland sought by boat and river the sites to build their manors and raise their families, these sites now are quite sequestered from the eye of the casual motorist. "Myrtle Grove" another of those Maryland family shrines, never passed from the possession of the descendants of the founder, having housed the Goldsborough family for over two hundred years, shrinks well protected from the public eye. It is located on a charming promontory between the Miles River and Goldsborough Creek. The paneled walls, the stairway, the cornices, the mantels and the simple elegance throughout the house are all that are necessary to endear it to those lovers of the traditions of early American homes.*)

CANDIED CARROTS

Boil carrot, scrape, cut in long thin strips as French fried potatoes are cut. Put in baking dish with brown sugar and butter, as sweet potatoes are candied.—*Mrs. Lewin W. Wickes, Kent County.*

BELL FRITTERS

Put a piece of butter the size of an egg into a pint of water, let it boil a few minutes, thicken it very smoothly with a pint of flour, let it remain a short time on the fire, stir it all the time lest it stick to the pan, pour it into a bowl and let it get cold. Add 6 eggs, breaking one at a time, beating it in until all are beaten in and the dough is quite light. Put a pint of lard in a pan and let it boil and then drop this batter in. The fritters when brown and crisp to be served up hot.—*Mrs. Robert Goldsborough Henry, Myrtle Grove, Talbot County.*

FRESH LIMA BEANS

Wash the beans and put on to cook in cold water, add about one-half teaspoon of sugar and a little butter, then add a little thickening of about half a teaspoon of flour mixed with a little cream. Salt and pepper to taste.—*Mrs. Joseph C. Byron, Washington County.*

CAULIFLOWER

Clean the cauliflowers well, but do not separate the head, boil it with a little salt in the water until tender. Have ready one tablespoon of flour worked in two tablespoonfuls of butter, half a pint of cream, pepper and salt. Make it hot enough to cook the flour, then put in the cauliflower after pressing the water out well and stew it until tender.—*Mr. and Mrs. George R. Dennis, Mt. Hampton, Frederick County.*

EASTERN SHORE STYLE BROCCOLI

Look over broccoli, wash thoroughly, cook about one pound of fat pork until tender. Add one peck of broccoli. Add teaspoonful of salt, and one-half teaspoonful of soda. Boil quickly until tender, drain, pepper and serve hot.—*Mrs. Harry A. Beach, Wicomico County.*

CORN PUDDING

1 quart of fresh corn and grate it so that the husk sticks to the grater.

Then add two whole eggs, well beaten, and butter the size of a teaspoon, then one tablespoon of sugar, and salt and pepper to taste.

Last add one-half cup of cream (if the cream is too heavy put in a little milk). Put into a hot oven and brown for about fifteen minutes.—*Mrs. Joseph C. Byron, Washington County.*

STUFFED EGGPLANT

Remove the stem from the eggplant and cut it in half lengthwise. Boil in salted water until the meaty inside of the eggplant is tender enough to be scooped out with a spoon, leaving the shell intact for stuffing. To the eggplant thus removed, add any left-over meat, preferably lamb, a small amount of cooked rice, some seeded raisins and salt and pepper to taste, mixing all well. Pack the mixture into the shell, holding it carefully, and place in a buttered shallow baking dish. On top put rolled cracker crumbs and several lumps of butter and bake in a moderate oven.—*Gerald W. Johnson, Baltimore.*

DISCOVERY OF A NEW DISH

"The discovery of a new dish confers more happiness on humanity, than the discovery of a new star."—Brillat-Savarin.

MACARONI

Boil one-half pound of Italian macaroni in milk and water until soft, not broken, drain and cool it on a sieve, and scrape or grate one-quarter pound of good cheese; put alternatingly in your dish, layers of macaroni and cheese with small lumps of butter. Season with nicely made mustard and cayenne pepper. Bake it for fifteen to twenty minutes.—*Miss Rebecca Hollingsworth French, Washington County.*

GREEN CORN IN IMITATION OF FRIED OYSTERS

One pint of green corn grated and pounded fine, one teacup of flour, one teacup of butter, four eggs, one tablespoonful of fine salt, one tablespoonful of pepper, mix them all together and fry it in butter, or nice lard, the same as oysters.—*Miss Rebecca Hollingsworth French, Washington County.*

CORN CHAFING DISH

(5 persons)

Four ears of good corn, one pint cream, one-half pound of butter, one-half a teaspoon salt, one teaspoon sugar. Boil corn on cob, cut off and place in chafing dish with cream, salt, butter and pepper until it begins to thicken.—*Hotel Rennert, Baltimore.*

SPANISH RICE

2 cupfuls cooked rice, 2 tablespoonfuls fat, 1 tablespoonful chopped onion, 2 tablespoonfuls chopped green pepper, 1½ cupfuls canned tomatoes, 1 tablespoonful capers, 1 tablespoonful mushrooms, ¼ teaspoonful salt. Buttered crumbs, cayenne, grated cheese.

Chop onion, pepper, and mushrooms, add to melted fat together with capers and seasonings and cook until onion browns. Add tomatoes and cook until moisture is nearly evaporated. Arrange alternate layers of rice and tomato mixture in a well-greased baking dish. Cover with buttered crumbs and grated cheese. Bake until heated through and crumbs are brown. Serves six.—*Mrs. J. H. Windsor, Windsor Manor, Baltimore County.*

CYMLINGS

Cut up young tender cymlings in a little salted water. Boil until soft enough to mash through a colander. Add tablespoon of butter, teaspoon of chopped onion, salt and pepper and one tablespoon of flour mixed with one-half cup milk. Put in baking dish. Cover with bread crumbs and dot with butter and bake to light brown.—*Mrs. John H. Sothoron, The Plains, St. Mary's County.*

CORN PATTIES

Take six ears corn, cut through center of grain lengthwise, then cut from cob raw, and scrape cob well, add to this one well-beaten egg, salt and pepper, one tablespoon melted butter, two tablespoons flour, two tablespoons milk, one teaspoon baking powder. Drop in hot fat and drain on paper. Serve very hot.—*Mrs. John H. Sothoron, The Plains, St. Mary's County.*

MUSHROOMS STEWED

To be peeled, washed, put into a stew pan with a piece of butter the size of an egg, one or two dusts of white flour. Season with black pepper and salt. When first put on stir them to prevent burning until they yield juice sufficient to cook them. Cook at least ¾ hour or until tender. Cook a silver spoon in them. If the spoon becomes black the mushrooms must not be eaten.—*Mrs. Charles H. Tilghman, Gross' Coate, Talbot County.*

CORN FRITTERS

One can corn or equivalent of fresh corn (when available). One cup flour; one teaspoonful (full measure) baking powder; one-quarter teaspoonful salt; one egg.

Mix all ingredients and fry slowly in well-greased pan. Serve with maple syrup.—*Mrs. Blanch Haulenbeek, Deep Creek Lake, Garrett County.*

SPAGHETTI

(6 persons)

Fry and brown in pure olive oil two onions, three sections of garlic and a half-green pepper sliced fine. Take out and set aside. Fry in olive oil a pound and a half of ground beef. Stew in separate pan three cans of tomato paste, diluting with same amount of water. Add one large can of highest grade Maryland tomatoes crushed through a colander. When tomato paste and tomatoes have come to a boil add the ground beef and onions, salt and pepper to taste, with addition of one-half teaspoonful of ground chilli. Let this simmer after well stirred from an hour and a half to two hours.

Boil three to four pounds of spaghetti fifteen minutes, adding salt to the water. Drain through colander; add sauce and mix well with a wooden spoon.

Serve finely grated parmesan cheese at table.—*Mrs. Frederick P. Stieff, Baltimore.*

GERMAN FRIED POTATOES

Peel and slice thin your raw potatoes. Drop in hot grease, season with salt and pepper to taste, let fry slowly until brown. Add about a gill of cream while frying and cover with lid. Turn off gas if gas stove is used, or if coal stove set on back part of stove until ready to serve.—*John Charles Thomas, Baltimore.*

HOMINY CHAFING DISH

(8 persons)

Three pints cold cooked hominy, one pint cream, one quarter pound butter, two teaspoons sugar, one-half teaspoon salt.

Place hominy, butter, salt and pepper in chafing dish with gill of cream, keep stirring and as hominy begins to thicken add balance of cream.—*Hotel Rennert, Baltimore.*

SAUERKRAUT

We make our winter's supply of kraut in the fall from the fall cabbage. A twenty-gallon crock jar will hold about one hundred and twenty-five pounds of cabbage shavings. These shavings are cut coarser than for cold slaw. Put one layer—about two gallons—of slaw in bottom. Pound with wooden mallet until juice forms on top. Then add about a handful of coarse salt, and a tablespoon of sugar with every two-gallon layer of kraut. Each layer should be thoroughly pounded until the juice rises on top. Then put a layer of cabbage leaves on top about an inch thick. We take a circular board so cut to fit freely inside the crock and weight it down with a large clean smooth stone. Put in warm place until fermentation ceases. Should be ready for use in about five or six weeks.—*Miss Zaidee Browning, Garrett County.*

HOT SLAW

One small head cabbage cut fine, cover with water and boil about fifteen minutes. All the water should be absorbed. Cover with dressing made as follows:

1 egg well beaten, 1 cup sour cream or 1 small can of condensed milk, vinegar, salt, pepper, sugar, and mustard to taste. Cook until thick, and put in a lump of butter before taking from the fire.—*Eleanor Birnie, Carroll County.*

BAKED PEPPERS

Remove stems and seeds from green or red peppers. Fill with tomatoes chopped fine, one-third as many onions, one-fourth as much fine bread crumbs, chopped celery, or celery leaves. Season to taste with salt, cayenne pepper and sugar. Put in uncovered baking dish, well greased, bake rather slowly until thoroughly cooked.—*Eleanor Birnie, Carroll County.*

"It is a curious fact that almost all the great artists in this line . . . seldom stay with the same employer . . . Is it that they sigh like the Macedonian for new worlds to conquer?"—"The Art of Dining"—Hayward.

BOILED POKE GREENS

The first shoot of the pokeberry plant six to eight inches tall. Wash thoroughly in cold water, do not remove leaves or stem. Put in pot with cold water and cook about a half an hour until done.

Put in colander and drain, and serve hot with melted butter, pepper, salt, or drawn butter, or Hollandaise sauce.—*Mrs. Symington Dawson (Mary Harris, Cook), Baltimore.*

SPINACH TIMBALES

(8 persons)

Pick over and wash carefully one-half peck spinach. Cook in uncovered kettle about ten minutes or until tender. Remove from fire and drain well. Season with salt, pepper, butter and grated horse-radish and a dash of nutmeg. Chop fine and pack in well-oiled molds. Unmold and garnish with hard-boiled eggs sprinkled with grated cheese and paprika. Serve very hot.—*Mrs. J. H. Windsor, Windsor Manor, Baltimore County.*

SWEET POTATO CROQUETTES

Bake the sweet potatoes until they are tender; then scoop out the centers and put them through a vegetable press. To each two cups of mashed potatoes allow a tablespoonful of butter, a level teaspoonful of salt, a tablespoonful of sugar and a half a salt-spoonful of white pepper; mix thoroughly. Form into cylinders, dip in egg, then in bread crumbs and fry in smoking hot fat.—*Miss Eliza Thomas, Baltimore.*

CANDIED SWEET POTATOES

Boil six sweet potatoes and peel. Cook until nearly done in boiling salted water. Drain, cut in halves, lengthwise, and put in a pan. Make a syrup of one-half cup water, one cup brown sugar and a lump of butter about the size of an egg. Cover potatoes with the syrup, put back in oven and bake until done, basting occasionally.—*Mrs. E. W. Humphreys, Wicomico County.*

SWEET POTATO PONE

Scrape or grate four large potatoes very fine, separate all the stringy particles. Beat up four eggs and stir with them a tablespoonful of butter, a teacup of cream; brown sugar, mace, ginger and nutmeg to taste. Bake in a tin pan well buttered; when cold turn out.—*Mrs. Wm. D. Poultney, Baltimore.*

BAKED TOMATOES

Scoop the pulp from whole, ripe tomatoes. Stuff the tomatoes with a filling made of the finely chopped pulp, one-third as many onions (chopped), one-fourth as many small bread crumbs, chopped celery or celery leaves. Season to taste with salt, pepper and sugar. Put in uncovered baking dish, well greased; bake rather slowly until thoroughly cooked.—*Eleanor Birnie, Carroll County.*

TURNIP GREENS AND HOG'S JOWL MARYLAND

Put about three pounds of hog jowl on with water and cook until tender. Remove hog's jowl, and add one peck of turnip greens which have been picked and washed, one teaspoon of salt and a half teaspoonful soda. Boil quickly until tender, drain, cut up pepper and serve hot with hog's jowl.—*Mrs. Harry A. Beach, Wicomico County.*

SALADS AND SALAD DRESSINGS

First Doughboy: *"How did you catch such a cold?"*
Second Doughboy: *"Somebody played the 'Star-Spangled Banner' while I was taking a bath."*

CHEESE SALAD

1 envelope gelatine, ½ cup cold water, 1 cup hot water, 2 cakes cream cheese, 1 cup mayonnaise, 1 can tomato soup, ¼ teaspoon salt, dash of red pepper, 1 onion chopped fine, ¾ cup

celery, chopped fine, 1 small bottle stuffed olives, chopped. Dissolve gelatine in cold water, when dissolved add hot water. Mix cheese, mayonnaise, salt, pepper, then add soup and gelatine. Chill slightly and add chopped onion, celery and olives.—*Mrs. Marion T. Hargis, Worcester County.*

BOILED SALAD DRESSING

This is best made with a double boiler or *bain-maire*.

The yolks and whites of three eggs are beaten separately and stirred in the boiler with one cup of cream or rich milk, one quarter teacup of vinegar, one teaspoonful each of mustard and pepper.

Cook slowly and when thick stir in two teaspoonsful of salt. If too thick, thin with more cream, melted butter or oil. Butter or oil can be used instead of cream, using more milk to keep it from being too hard.

Stir constantly when boiling and when cooling to make it smooth.—*D. Charles Winebrener, Frederick County.*

FROZEN CHEESE SALAD

One can crushed pineapple (pint), well drained. One small bottle of maraschino cherries, chopped and drained. Three tablespoons XXXX sugar. Chill one hour. Mash one package cream cheese, mix with three-quarter cup Mayonnaise dressing. Add the chilled fruit, then fold in one gill of cream, whipped. Pack and freeze like a mousse. Serve on lettuce.—*Mrs. C. P. Brundige, Court Place, Carroll County.*

"OLD BAY LINE"—BALTO. STEAM PACKET CO., EST. 1840

EASTERN SHORE SALAD

Ingredients: Celery, shrimp, crab meat, olives, capers, cress, hard-boiled eggs, ripe olives. On leaves of lettuce, place equal quantities of small shrimp (cleaned) and large crab flakes, mix crab meat with mayonnaise in a small mound and circle shrimp around it, place a few chopped capers and ripe olives mixed together in mayonnaise in center of each shrimp; garnish with quartered hard-boiled eggs, on which a little paprika is placed.—*Mr. H. B. Grimshaw, Baltimore Steam Packet Co., Baltimore.*

ROQUEFORT CHEESE DRESSING

To one cup of French dressing use two à la carte portions of Roquefort cheese; the cheese to be mashed, and worked well into the French dressing. Add a half demi-tasse of cream into same with juice of half a lemon.—*Dining Car Service, B. & O. R. R.*

CHICKEN SALAD

Boil one 5-pound fat chicken. When cooked remove it from vessel and let the liquor in which it was cooked cool. Chop the meat of the chicken fine, adding one-half as much celery as chicken.

Dressing: Use 6 hard-boiled eggs, remove the yolks and mash; skim the fat from the liquor in which the chicken was cooked, mix it carefully in the yolks of the eggs, season with salt, pepper, and paprika to taste. Mix dressing into the chicken and celery, garnish with the white of eggs, sliced.—*General Francis E. Waters, Baltimore.*

COLD SLAW

Chop or shred a small head of cabbage and crisp same in ice water. Add three tablespoonsful of minced celery if desired.

Dressing: 1 tablespoon oil, 4 tablespoons vinegar, 1 teaspoonful mixed mustard, 1 teaspoonful salt, 1 teaspoonful sugar, ½ teaspoonful pepper. Pour over slaw just before serving and mix well.—*Mrs. W. T. Hamilton, Washington County.*

MOLDED PINEAPPLE SALAD

One pint can of crushed pineapple. One cup sugar (granulated). Juice of one lemon. Bring to a boil and add to it one envelope of gelatine previously soaked in one-quarter cup of cold water. Let cool and add 2 packages of cream cheese. Mix well. When entirely cooled, add one pint of whipped cream. Pour in cold wet molds.—*Mrs. C. P. Brundige, Carroll County.*

JELLIED CHICKEN SALAD

Use chicken stock that has been in refrigerator long enough so all fat can be removed from top. Heat one pint this stock to boiling point, dissolve one envelope Knox's gelatine with one-third cup of cold water. Pour over it the boiling stock and add three-quarters cup vinegar (or one-half of tarragon vinegar), juice of lemon, salt to taste. When nearly congealed add two cups chicken, one cup celery, one cup olives and pimentos mixed and a little green pepper and parsley. Asparagus tips can be used in mold.—*Miss Mary McDaniel, Talbot County.*

MAYONNAISE DRESSING
(*Cooked*)

3 eggs, 3 heaping teaspoons flour, 3 teaspoons sugar, 1 teaspoon salt, ½ teaspoon mustard, 2 cups diluted vinegar, red pepper, butter size of a small egg. Cook in double boiler and stir constantly until it thickens.—*Mrs. Nora D. Bratten, Worcester County.*

PINEAPPLE SALAD

1 pt. pineapple, 1 box marshmallows cut in small pieces, 1 cup whipped cream, English walnuts or pecans.

Dressing: Yolks of two eggs, 2 tablespoons vinegar, ¾ tablespoon butter, 1/3 tablespoon sugar. Cook in double boiler, stirring constantly, until it begins to thicken. When cold, mix with cup of whipped cream and serve.—*Mrs. Nora D. Bratten, Worcester County.*

"Cooking is the most ancient of the arts, for Adam was born hungry."—
BRILLAT-SAVARIN.

TOMATO ASPIC RING, FOR CHICKEN SALAD

Heat one cup tomato juice with one onion sliced, a bay-leaf, a few whole black peppers. Strain over two tablespoonsful gelatine soaked in ½ cup cold water. Blend an additional 1½ cups tomato juice with two packages cream cheese. Combine the two mixtures and season with salt to taste. Cool and when beginning to thicken add 1 cup of cream whipped very stiff. Chill until solid. Unmold on large platter and fill ring with chicken salad made according to your favored receipt. Surround with lettuce cups filled with more salad. Serve with mayonnaise and cheese straws.—*Mrs. J. H. Windsor, Windsor Manor, Baltimore County.*

172

OLD-FASHIONED POTATO SALAD

Boil eight small potatoes in jackets. When done remove from water at once. When cool peel and cut in thin round slices. Add: ½ teaspoonful salt, a little pepper, 1 tablespoonful chopped parsley. Boil ½ pint vinegar with 1 tablespoonful sugar and 1 tablespoonful butter. Pour over potatoes. Add celery seed and green peppers if desired. Add two hard-boiled eggs sliced thin.— *Mrs. Ida Kenney, Baltimore.*

JELLIED VEGETABLE SALAD

1 package lime-flavored gelatine, 3 medium-sized carrots, grated, 1 medium-sized onion, grated, 1 tomato cut fine, 1 green pepper chopped, 4 large stalks celery cut fine, 1 tablespoon vinegar, 1 lemon. Salt, cayenne and grated horse-radish.

Peel carrots and grate; add to grated onion, chopped tomato, pepper and celery. Add juice of lemon and season with salt, cayenne and horse-radish. Prepare lime gelatine according to standard method on box and cool; when beginning to thicken stir in the vinegar and the vegetables. Pour in one large or individual molds.—*Mrs. J. H. Windsor, Windsor Manor, Baltimore County.*

MEXICAN SLAW

Prepare cabbage the same as for cold slaw. Dice cold ham, cold tongue, green peppers and pimentos. Mix all together, thin mayonnaise with sweet cream, add small amount of sugar, pour the dressing over the slaw and serve on lettuce leaves.—*Dining Car Service, B. & O. R. R.*

SAUCES

DAMSON SAUCE

Allow one-half pound of brown sugar to every pound of fruit and to each seven pounds of fruit mixture add one pint of strong vinegar; let cook slowly so as not to break skins. Take up in jar, put cloves in syrup, boil and pour over fruit.—*Mrs. J. Morsell Roberts, Calvert County.*

BRANDY SAUCE

Four eggs, one-half cupful of butter, one cupful of sugar, three tablespoonsful of brandy, six tablespoonsful of hot water. Butter and sugar are creamed together. Add well-beaten yolks of four eggs. Add hot water a little at a time. Add brandy last. Pour sauce in serving dish and put well-beaten whites of the four eggs on top. Mix the whites into the sauce as you serve it over the prepared pudding, cake or Brown Betty.—*Mrs. Emerson C. Harrington, Jr., Dorchester County.*

APPLE SAUCE

Peel apples and slice in quarters. Stew in not too much water, mash and sweeten. Season with cinnamon to taste. Yellow transparent apples preferred.—*John Charles Thomas, Baltimore.*

BUTTER SCOTCH SAUCE

One and one-half cups brown sugar, three tablespoons butter, one-half can Blue Label Karo Syrup, cook until it threads, remove from fire and stir in one-half cup thin cream—*Miss Mary McDaniel, Talbot County.*

"Les écrivains-cuisiniers sont aussi necessaires que les autres littérateurs; il vous faut connaître la du plus ancien des arts."—CHARLES GIRARD.

BÉCHAMEL SAUCE

Mix cold and well together in a tin sauce-pan two ounces of butter and a tablespoonful of flour, then add a pint of milk and set on the fire; stir continually and when turning rather thick take off; beat up the yolk of an egg in a cup with a teaspoonful of water, turn into the sauce and mix well again; salt and pepper to taste and it is ready for use.—*Dr. Walter Forman Wickes, Wickliffe, Greenspring Valley, Baltimore County.*

CREAM GRAVY

Tablespoonful of flour and water, enough to make a thin paste. Pour over chicken and add, while simmering, about a pint of milk and cream mixed.—*John Charles Thomas, Baltimore.*

SAUCE FOR BOILED ROCK FISH

Two heaping tablespoonsful of flour mixed with water. Add the yolks of two eggs and beat well. Stir into this a pint of boiling water. Cook until thickened. Just before removing from stove add half pint of milk and two hard-boiled eggs sliced or minced, and a piece of butter the size of an egg. Put the fish on a platter and serve while hot.—*Mrs. Charles Wickes Whaland, Kent County.*

FOAMY SAUCE

1 cup sugar, 1 tablespoon water, ½ cup butter, 1 egg, 1 tablespoon cooking sherry, 1 tablespoon vanilla.

Directions: Put the sugar, water, and butter in a saucepan. Allow them to melt but not to boil. Beat the yolk and pour the melted butter, sugar and water into the yolk, stirring continuously. Add sherry and vanilla. Beat the white until stiff and add it and beat the whole mixture until it is foamy.

Sauce is for French toast (the kind dipped in milk and then in egg and fried in butter) or for plum pudding. Cut bread about ⅜ inch and trim with a cookie cutter, soak in milk and then dip in beaten egg and fry in butter.—*Emily Post, Author of "Etiquette" and "The Personality of a House," etc.*

ROSE WATER

Fill any size bottle *full* of rose leaves as it can hold, then fill it with alcohol and set it in the sun.—*Mrs. George H. Birnie, Carroll County.*

SAUCE HOLLANDAISE

2 tablespoons of butter, ½ pint of boiling water, 1 tablespoon of flour.

Cream butter and flour in bowl. Put on fire, add hot water gradually until it thickens and stir. Take from fire, when thick add yolks of 2 eggs well beaten, but gradually. Add 1 teaspoonful of onion juice, if desired juice of ½ lemon, 1 tablespoon of chopped parsley, 1 teaspoon of salt and pepper to taste.—*John Ridgely, Hampton, Baltimore County.*

SAUCE HOLLANDAISE

Heat in a saucepan two slices of onion, two bay-leaves, a saltspoonful of celery seed and six tablespoonsful of vinegar. When reduced one-half, strain and cool. Rub together one tablespoonful of butter and one of flour; add a half pint of boiling water and stir until boiling.

Take from the fire, add the yolks of two eggs, beaten; reheat; add a tablespoonful of butter cut in small blocks, half a teaspoonful of salt, a dash of pepper and the vinegar.

This is a most excellent sauce for fish.—*D. Charles Winebrener, Frederick County.*

LEMON BUTTER

Beat three eggs briskly. Juice of three lemons and grated rind of one. 2½ cups of sugar beaten until light in eggs. Add lemon juice and rind, one-half teaspoon butter. Cook in double boiler until thick enough to use as spread.—*Mrs. Nell C. Westcott, Kent County.*

"Salt yo' food, suh, with humor . . . season it with wit, and sprinkle it all over with the charm of good-fellowship, but never poison it with the cares of yo' life. It is an insult to yo' digestion, besides bein', suh, a mark of bad breedin'."
—*"Col. Carter of Cartersville,"* F. HOPKINSON SMITH.

SAUCE FOR PLUM PUDDING

(As made in the home of Gov. Thomas Nelson of Yorktown, Virginia)

One-half pound of brown sugar, a quarter pound of butter creamed, heat over hot water until liquid, add to one beaten egg, cook until it thickens. Then add a wineglass of wine and some nutmeg and serve at once.—*Mr. Alexander C. Nelson, Baltimore.*

RASPBERRY VINEGAR

Bruise a quart of fresh gathered fruit in a clean bowl, pour over it a pint of good vinegar and cover closely. Let stand 3 days and stir daily. Strain through flannel bag. Let drip but do not squeeze. To a pint of the liquor put one pound of sugar (receipt says loaf pounded). Boil 10 (ten) minutes and skim well. When cold bottle and cork tightly. A glass of brandy added to one quart of vinegar improves it.—*Mrs. Robert Goldsborough Henry, Myrtle Grove, Talbot County.*

MINT SAUCE

(Old Receipt)

Mix one tablespoonful of sugar in half cup of good vinegar. Add green mint and let it infuse for half an hour in cold place before straining and sending to table. Serve with roast lamb.— *Mrs. Frank L. Bentz, Washington County.*

WINE SAUCE

One-quarter pound butter, six large tablespoonsful of brown sugar, one egg, one glass wine (or more).

Beat butter and sugar to a cream, add egg and beat until light, put in wine gradually. Cook until thick and nearly boiling. Stir constantly.—*Mrs. George H. Birnie, Carroll County.*

BREADS

BACHELOR'S LOAF

FOUR eggs—whites and yolks beaten separately as for sponge cake —two pints of cornmeal, one teaspoonful of salt; pour into this four pints of boiling milk and water mixed with one quarter pound butter melted into it, add the yolks, then the whites, bake in a quick oven.

One-half this quantity makes one usual loaf.—*Dr. Walter Forman Wickes, Wickcliffe, Greenspring Valley, Baltimore County.*

DATE BISCUIT

2 cups flour, 4 teaspoonsful baking powder, ½ cup chopped dates, 4 tablespoons shortening, 1 teaspoon salt, 2/3 cup milk. Mix flour, baking powder and salt; work in shortening, then add dates and milk. When mixed turn onto floured board and roll or pat to about one-half inch thickness and cut with small cutter. —*Mrs. J. H. Windsor, Windsor Manor, Baltimore County.*

MARYLAND BISCUITS

½ pint flour, 1/3 teaspoonful salt, 1/3 tablespoonful lard. Add salt to the flour, then rub in lard thoroughly with hands; put ½ gill milk and ½ gill water in pitcher and add slowly to flour, stirring and kneading all the time; *the flour should be just moistened,* for dough must be very stiff. Knead five minutes and beat with hatchet thirty minutes; make in small biscuits and stick with fork on top; bake in moderate oven for twenty minutes.— *Mrs. J. Douglas Freeman, Baltimore.*

MARYLAND BEATEN BISCUIT

3 pints winter wheat flour, ¼ lb. lard, one-half ice water and milk to make a stiff dough, 1 heaping teaspoonful salt. Work in the lard, add the liquid and beat with a club for twenty-five minutes. Make in small biscuits and bake in a hot oven.—*Mrs. Charles Sterett Grason, Cornwalys Cross Manor, St. Mary's County.*

MARYLAND DROP BISCUITS

2 cups flour, 4 teaspoons baking powder, ½ teaspoon salt, 2 tablespoons shortening.

Method: Mix and sift flour, salt and baking powder, cut in the shortening, add enough milk or water so the mixture will drop from a spoon. Drop in muffin tins and bake in a hot oven 12 or 15 minutes.—*Mrs. Howard W. Jackson, Baltimore.*

OLD-FASHIONED PIN WHEEL BISCUITS

2 cups flour, 4 teaspoons baking powder, ½ teaspoon salt, 2 tablespoons butter, 2/3 cup milk.

Filling: 4 tablespoons brown sugar, 2 tablespoons butter, 1/3 teaspoon cinnamon, 1/3 cup chopped raisins.

Method: Mix as for drop biscuits, add milk gradually to make soft dough. Toss dough on floured board and roll lightly ¼ inch thick; spread with melted butter, cinnamon, sugar and fruit. Roll like a jelly roll, cut in pieces ¾ inch thick, place on greased pan and bake 12 or 15 minutes. Sprinkle with powdered sugar.—*Mrs. Howard W. Jackson, Baltimore.*

"The finest landscape in the world is improved by a good inn in the fore-ground."—SAMUEL JOHNSON.

ALMOND BREAD

Blanch and pound in a mortar one-half pound shelled sweet almonds till they are a smooth paste, adding rose water as you pound them. They should be done the day before they are wanted. Prepare a pound of loaf sugar finely powdered, a teaspoonful of mixed spice (mace, cinnamon) and three-quarters of a pound of sifted flour. Take fourteen eggs and separate the whites from the yolks, leaving out seven of the whites, and beat the other seven to a stiff froth. Beat the yolks till very thick, and smooth and then put the sugar gradually into them, adding the spice. Next stir in the white of eggs, then the flour and lastly the almonds. You may add twelve drops of the essence of lemon. Put the mixture into a square tin pan (well buttered) or into a

187

copper or tin pan. Mold and set it immediately in a brick oven. Ice it when cool. It is best eaten fresh.—*Mrs. James Bordley, Jr., Baltimore.*

CORN BREAD

One cup corn meal, one-quarter cup flour, two tablespoons sugar, one large teaspoonful baking powder, one egg, three tablespoonsful of melted shortening, salt to taste and two cups of milk. Mix thoroughly and bake.—*Mrs. W. B. Deen, Caroline County.*

DATE AND NUT BREAD

One pound of stoned dates; one-half pound of Brazil nuts; one-half pound English walnuts; one cup of flour; one teaspoonful of salt; two large teaspoonsful of baking powder. Sift flour, salt, baking powder together three times; add one cup of granulated sugar and mix again. Four eggs, whites beaten stiff; bake one hour in slow oven.—*Mrs. Wm. H. Thomas, Carroll County.*

DIXIE BREAD

1 quart of corn meal, 2 full teaspoonsful salt, 1 quart boiling water. Mix well and set aside to cool. Add about a half teacup of yeast (1 yeast cake), if weak a little more. Add little less than a quart of flour. Knead. Pat down in bowl, sprinkle a little flour on top and put in a warm place to rise. When ready to use put a little flour on the board and cut off a spoonful of dough. Roll into shape, flatten with a spoon and bake on the bottom of the oven.—*Mrs. Charles B. Trail, Frederick County.*

BREAD

Two scant quarts of Ceresota flour, two tablespoons of salt, two tablespoons of sugar, three-quarters of a cup of lard, one yeast cake dissolved in warm water. Mix sugar and salt through the flour, then well work in lard. Add the dissolved yeast and enough warm water to make a soft dough. Stand overnight to lighten well. Make into loaves with as little kneading as possible. Lighten again, and when almost double in size bake in a moderate oven for one hour or longer.—*Mollie Howard Ash, Cecil County.*

FEDERAL BREAD

(Sometimes called Irish Bread)

¾ cup milk, ½ cup yeast (1 yeast cake), 2 eggs, lard size of small egg, 1 full tablespoon sugar, 3 cups flour. Melt lard in milk and pour slowly to the beaten eggs; add salt and other ingredients; set aside to rise, pour in baking tin with vent in the center (old-fashioned cake tin), let rise again and bake in moderate oven ¾ hour at least.—*Mrs. Nora D. Bratten, Worcester County.*

TYRONE BUNS

Three-quarters of a pound of white sugar; six ounces of butter; four eggs; one and one-half cups of sweet milk; one teaspoonful of cream of tartar. Then dissolve one teaspoonful of soda in a little milk. Take as much flour as you think desired. Roll into bun shape and bake.—*Mrs. Wm. H. Thomas, Carroll County.*

TANEY KITCHEN, FREDERICK

SOFT GINGER BREAD

(THIS *receipt, as in the case of others from the same source, was used in the Taney family of Maryland during slavery days and was included in the old receipt book used by Mrs. Juliet Eliza Sollers Taney, whose husband, Dr. Augustine Taney, was the son of Joseph Taney, Uncle of Chief Justice Roger Brooke Taney.*
The original receipt book is owned by Miss Lelia Taney and Miss Alice Taney, granddaughters of Dr. and Mrs. Augustine Taney.)

Add one pound of butter to a quart of molasses, three pounds of flour, ginger and orange peel to your taste, potash the size of a nutmeg. Let them stand near the fire while the oven is heating. Bake them in a quick oven.—*The Misses Lelia and Alice Taney, Frederick County.*

NUT BREAD

Mix well:—one egg, one cupful brown sugar, one cupful sweet milk, two cupfuls flour and two teaspoonsful baking powder. Add a cupful of chopped or broken walnut meats, slightly floured. Turn into a buttered loaf pan and let stand for about fifteen minutes and then place in a moderate oven and bake for about a half to three-quarters of an hour, or until the bread does not stick when tried in the center with a straw and also recedes from the sides of the pan.—*J. Butterfield, Proprietor, The Country Club Inn, Harford County.*

SPOON BREAD

Two cups of grits or small hominy or rice boiled, 1 teaspoonful of salt, thin while hot, put in a piece of butter the size of an egg. Four eggs. Beat the yolks and the whites of the eggs separately, thin the grits with milk until it is like thick cream, stir in the yolks of the eggs and half a pint of corn meal. Fold in the whites of the eggs last and bake in a deep buttered dish about three-quarters of an hour. Cover if it browns too fast.—*Mrs. Charles Sterett Grason, Cornwalys Cross Manor, Beachville, St. Mary's County.*

BUCKWHEAT CAKES

One-half pint milk; one-half pint buttermilk; one-quarter yeast cake dissolved in milk; one-half teaspoonful salt.

Add to this enough buckwheat flour to make it the consistency of hot cake batter. This should be allowed to stand all night. In the morning, before making the cakes, scald one-quarter teaspoonful of baking soda and add to the mixture. If not sweet enough, add more soda. The batter is usually made and kept in a regular buckwheat jug or stone pitcher, and may be added to as needed.—*Mrs. Blanche Haulenbeek, Deep Creek Lake, Garrett County.*

CROSS MANOR

GRANT, SEPTEMBER 8TH, 1633.   HOUSE BUILT 1642

("CROSS MANOR," *oldest house in Maryland, built by Sir Thomas Cornwalys, Lieutenant Governor of the Province under Leonard Calvert, Lord Baltimore, called originally "Cornwalys Cross." The grant was 4000 acres. The lineal descendant as Mistress of the Manor today is Mrs. Rose Ellicott Grason, through her mother's lineage, Jones, also Capt. John Morris Ellicott, U.S.N. The name "Cross" derived from the planting of a cross to a friend who was killed by accident by Sir Thomas Cornwalys.)*

EDGEHILL MUFFINS

1 quart of flour, 1 egg, piece of lard size of an egg, ½ cup of yeast, or half cake of yeast, salt, enough milk to make a stiff batter. Beat egg, add lard, then yeast, sift in flour, beat all together. Set to rise. Drop from spoon into pan. Bake in hot oven.—*Miss Mary W. Crisfield, Somerset County.*

RISEN FLANNEL CAKES

1 quart flour, 1 teaspoonful salt, 2 eggs, 1 tablespoonful melted butter, 2 tablespoonsful sugar, ¼ cake yeast dissolved in warm milk with the sugar, thin with warm milk to the right consistency, set to rise one night in a warm place. In the morning add the beaten eggs and melted butter before baking.

Waffles and ring muffins can be made in the same way only have the batter *very* thin for waffles and thicker for muffins. —*Mrs. Charles Sterett Grason, Cornwalys Cross Manor, St. Mary's County.*

MARYLAND RICE BREAD

(THE *date of the erection of The Hermitage is unknown, but the land upon which it stands is part of a tract of 1400 acres which was patented to Nicholas Painter in 1681. The house is built of brick which was brought from England and is covered with plaster. The front of the house is three stories high but the back is only two stories. The partitions between the rooms are solid brick and are sixteen inches thick.*

During the Revolution the house was occupied by Robert Alexander, a Tory, who left with General Howe's fleet in 1777 and was never heard of again. For the past seventy years it has been owned and occupied by the Bratton family.)

1 cupful rice, boiled, 1 tablespoonful butter, 3 eggs beaten separately, 1 pint of milk, ½ pint meal, salt.

Stir into the rice while warm the butter and salt; mix yolks and milk together, add the meal, then the rice, and last of all the whites. Butter the dish and put in the batter, fill in the dish as full as it will hold as it bakes better. Put it in a hot oven, gradually lower the temperature until it is moderately hot, and bake for an hour and a quarter.—*Katherine M. Bratton, The Hermitage, Cecil County.*

ALMOND CHEESE CAKE

Sixty almonds, one half pound sugar, six eggs, leaving out two of the whites, one-half a nutmeg, a little wine, the peel of two lemons and not quite a half pound of butter.—*Mrs. James Bordley, Jr., Baltimore.*

RYE BREAD

2 quarts flour, 1 quart rye flour, 2 tablespoonsful salt, 2 tablespoonsful sugar, 2 tablespoonsful lard or butter, 1 yeast cake, 2 tablespoonsful kümmel seed, enough lukewarm water to make stiff dough.

Sift flour and make a well in center; add part of water and shortening, sugar and salt; dissolve yeast in half cup warm water. In kneading dough you can add the necessary water to get dough the right consistency. Let stand overnight in warm place; in morning make in loaves, put in greased pans, let stand to rise; it takes from one hour to an hour and a quarter to bake.—*Mrs. Ida Kenney, Baltimore.*

OLD MARYLAND CORN CAKES

Take fresh water-ground cornmeal and scald with boiling water to a thin batter. Salt to taste and fry on an iron griddle greased with fat ham or bacon rind. The consistency of the batter should be such as to run into a very thin cake with crisp brown edges. The meal should be of the coarse, old-fashioned variety, not the fine, bolted meal now generally sold.—*Frederic Arnold Kummer, Baltimore.*

CLABBER OR BUTTERMILK GRIDDLE CAKES

1 cup flour, 1 teaspoon salt, 1 teaspoon baking powder, 1 egg, 1½ cups clabber or buttermilk, ¾ teaspoon soda.

Break egg in bowl, beat and add about half the clabber, then sift in the flour with salt and baking powder and mix well, adding rest of clabber. Last add the soda dissolved in a little water. Fry.

(These are nice used as pancakes or fritters for dessert by adding fruit and serving with hard sauce.)—*Readbourne Receipts, Queen Anne's County (Courtesy Mr. Swepson Earle).*

CORN CAKES

(As made at Elkridge Club)

Three cups of cornmeal, one heaping tablespoonful of brown sugar, or two tablespoonsful of molasses, two eggs, one teaspoon salt, one-quarter cup of melted butter, three cups of milk. Have paste about as thick as thick cream. Have a very hot griddle, do not put in all the milk at first as all may not be needed.—*Mr. Alexander C. Nelson, Baltimore.*

JOHNNY CAKE

("Fit for an Alderman, Mayor, Editor, etc., or any dignitary of the land.")

One quart milk, three eggs, one teaspoonful saleratus, one teacup wheat flour, and Indian meal sufficient to make a batter consistency of pancakes. Bake quick—in pans, buttered—and eat warm with butter.—*Mrs. Robert Goldsborough Henry, Myrtle Grove, Talbot County.*

CORN PONE

Three eggs, one teaspoon of sugar, one cup of melted shortening (lard—roast beef or chicken fat), two cups of buttermilk, scant teaspoon of soda, three cups of corn meal. Sift dry ingredients together, beat eggs and sugar together, add milk and meal, lastly pour in the shortening. Bake in a hot oven fifteen or twenty minutes.—*Mrs. James H. Preston, Baltimore.*

INDIAN MUFFINS

Have ready a pint of sifted Indian meal (cornmeal or maize). Mix with a handful of wheat flour. Melt one-quarter pound of fresh butter in a quart of milk. Beat four eggs very light and stir into them alternately (a little at a time of each) the milk when it is quite cold and the meal putting in a small teaspoonful of salt, the whole must be beaten long and hard. Then butter some muffin irons and set them on a hot griddle and pour some of the batter into each. Send them to the table hot, and split them by pulling them open with your fingers as a knife will make them heavy.—*Miss Rebecca Hollingsworth French, Washington County.*

FRENCH PANCAKES

Two eggs, two ounces of butter, two ounces of flour, one ounce sugar, one-half pint of milk. Put flour in bowl, add sugar, melted butter, eggs and milk. Bake in buttered saucers for fifteen minutes and serve with hot sauce.—*Miss Louisa Ogle Thomas, Baltimore.*

ENGLISH MUFFINS

3 cups flour, 1 teaspoon salt, pinch of soda, 1 heaping teaspoon baking powder, 2 tablespoons sugar, 1 egg, 2/3 cup buttermilk. Sift together first four ingredients. Break egg into buttermilk, add sugar, mix thoroughly and sift in the flour. Beat until the consistency of cake batter, add shortening and mix thoroughly. Drop into hot, greased pan and bake.—*Mr. H. B. Grimshaw, Baltimore Steam Packet Co., Baltimore.*

EGG PONE

Pour one teacup full of hot rice, boiled soft, over one quart of meal. Add a piece of butter the size of an egg, one and a half pints of milk and three eggs well beaten. Bake in a dish one-half to three-quarters of an hour.—*Mrs. Bartlett S. Johnston, Baltimore.*

OLD-FASHIONED SUNDAY PONE

(Started Saturday)

5 lbs. meal, one tablespoonful salt, one cup sugar, one cup molasses, 2 qts. hot water, make thin enough to pour. Make up about ten o'clock in the morning and let stand until two (2) P.M. Bake all afternoon and when dinner is over permit to remain in warm oven overnight. This is a peculiarly characteristic dish of Worcester County and used to be made in a three-legged iron pot the lid of which had a deep rim so that hot coals could be placed upon it. The entire pot was surrounded with live coals and banked until ready for use Sunday morning.—*Mrs. Marion T. Hargis, Worcester County.*

MELFIELD

("MELFIELD," *built "before the Revolution," is one of those Manors of Mary-land that justifies one's belief of what the manor of a Southern gentleman should be. The spacious portico supported by four impressive fluted Doric columns blends the dignity of the Roman architecture with the informality and hospitality of an English homestead.*)

CUSTARD PONE

3 eggs well beaten, lard, a piece the size of a hen's egg, 1 teacup full of sifted cornmeal, 1 teaspoonful salt, 3 pints milk, 2 teaspoons yeast powder. After putting in the oven for five minutes, open and stir well, repeat again in five minutes, then bake. If your dish is just large enough for 1 quart of milk, do not put the cup of meal quite full.—*Swepson Earle, Betsy's receipt, Melfield, Queen Anne's County.*

SALLY LUNN

4 eggs, 1½ cups sugar, ¼ lb. butter, 1½ cups milk, 4 teacups flour, 3 even teaspoons baking powder. Cream butter and sugar together, add well-beaten eggs—add milk—then flour, baking powder and salt sifted together. Beat *well* and bake in tin with vent in the center in slow oven ¾ hour or about that amount of time depending on the individual oven.—*Mrs. Nora D. Bratten, Worcester County.*

ICE BOX ROLLS

¾ cup of butter and lard (mixed); ¼ cup of sugar (scant); 1 teaspoon salt; 1 cup of boiling water. Pour boiling water over butter and lard, when melted, add one cup of cold water, add sugar and salt. Beat well. Add 3 cups of flour and beat flour in well. Then add 2 eggs. Dissolve 2 yeast cakes in ¼ cup of lukewarm water and add 3 more cups of flour and mix thoroughly. Put in ice box and when you want to use them allow 3 hours for raising.—*Mrs. C. P. Brundige, Court Place, Carroll County.*

PULL OPENS

Put 1 yeast cake in 1 cup cold water. Rub 2/3 cup lard in 5 cups flour and 1 teaspoonful salt, 1 tablespoon sugar. Beat 2 eggs, add yeast cake water and 1 cupful hot water to flour. Let set in cool place until morning. In the morning pinch off this dough in pieces the size of an egg and cook slowly in hot lard on top of stove.—*Mrs. Lewin W. Wickes, Kent County.*

PARTRIDGE HILL

("Partridge Hill" *was built by Colonel Henry Hollingsworth, of Elkton, Chief Commissary for General Washington. This beautiful Colonial home is situated on Main Street, Elkton [formerly the old Post Road between Baltimore and Philadelphia]. It is now owned by Mrs. Elva Gilpin Denney, in whose family it has remained for many years.*)

PARKER HOUSE ROLLS

1 pint of cold boiled milk, 1 teaspoonful of salt, 2 quarts of sifted flour, 1 large spoonful of lard, 1 teaspoonful of sugar, ½ cup of yeast or half a compressed cake dissolved in a half-cup of lukewarm water.

Put the flour into a deep bowl, add salt and sugar. Mix and then rub in the lard. Make a well in the center. Mix the yeast and milk together, put it into the well, and let it stand until morning. Then stir and knead thoroughly, first in the bowl, and, as soon as stiff enough, on the board. Now pound it for fifteen minutes with a potato masher; as soon as it becomes velvety, put it back in the bowl, cover it, and set away in a warm place (72 Fahr.) until very light. When light, roll out on the board a quarter-inch thick, cut with a round cutter, fold one-third over two-thirds, put on a greased baking sheet; let stand again one hour, bake in a quick oven (400 Fahr.) for fifteen minutes.

Remember that different kinds of flour require more or less moisture. Do not add the whole two quarts, if less will answer.—*Mrs. Elva Gilpin Denney, Partridge Hill, Cecil County.*

POPOVERS

1 pint milk, 2 eggs, 1 tablespoonful of butter, 1½ of flour, ½ teaspoon of salt. After beating very light, pour in the melted butter (a large tablespoonful) just before bakng. Fill this tin half full and bake in a hot oven.—*Miss Mary W. Crisfield, Somerset County.*

DEEVER ROLLS

One pint milk, one-half cup lard, one-half cup butter, one cup sugar, heaping teaspoonful salt, two eggs, one yeast cake. Heat milk warm enough for butter to melt, add yeast dissolved in warm water and flour to make thin batter, let rise, then add flour to a consistency of bread dough, let rise again, then roll out and cut for rolls or doughnuts. Let rise and bake in hot oven. —*Mrs. C. S. Gore, Baltimore.*

POTATO ROLLS

Two cupfuls mashed potatoes, one-half cupful lard, 1 yeast cake dissolved in one cup of water to which has been added one tablespoon of sugar. Salt. Flour to make soft dough. Put in a warm place to lighten. When light make into rolls and lighten again.—*Mrs. Nell C. Westcott, Kent County.*

RUSKS

How to make Rusks, Good Rusks, first rate: Beat seven eggs, mix them with half a pint of warm new milk, a quarter pound of butter that has been melted, add a quarter pint of yeast (1 yeast cake), and three ounces of sugar, put them gradually into as much flour as will make a light paste nearly as thin as batter. Let it rise before the fire half an hour, add more flour to make it a little stiffer, work it well and divide it into small loaves or cakes about five or six inches wide and flatten. When baked and cold put them in the oven to brown a little. Amen.—*Miss Julia Loker, Mulberry Fields, St. Mary's County.*

WAFFLES

About a quart of flour, scant teaspoonful of salt, tablespoonful of sugar, two tablespoonsful of Wesson oil, two eggs, and buttermilk. Mix flour, salt, sugar and buttermilk until a thin batter is formed. Then beat in well two tablespoonsful of Wesson oil and two eggs. Add soda and a little hot water.—*John Charles Thomas, Baltimore.*

RICE WAFFLES

Boil a half teacup of rice, the day before. Take eight eggs well beaten, the whites and yolks separately, one quart of rich milk, a tablespoonful of flour to each egg. Beat up the eggs first, then add the milk, rice and flour last. Stir in the flour gently and do not beat the mixture afterwards.—*Mrs. Charles H. Tilghman, Gross' Coate, Talbot County.*

CHOCOLATE WAFFLES

One-half cup butter, two teaspoonsful yeast powder, one cup sugar, one and one-half cups flour, two eggs, one-half cup milk, one-quarter teaspoonful salt, two ounces melted chocolate, vanilla to taste.

Cream butter and sugar, then add eggs well beaten. Sift flour, yeast powder and salt together and add alternating with milk. Stir in chocolate and vanilla. Bake on very hot waffle iron. Serve with whipped cream or XXXX sugar.—*Miss Mary McDaniel, Talbot County.*

CORN WAFFLES

Sift two cups of flour, one teaspoon salt, one tablespoonful of sugar and three teaspoonsful of baking powder into mixing bowl. Beat whites and yolks of two eggs separately, add two cups of milk to yolks and beat. Add this to sifted flour, beating until very smooth. Then add four tablespoons melted butter and one cup of fresh corn just off the cob and the stiffly beaten whites of eggs.—*Mrs. W. B. Deen, Caroline County.*

TEA ROLLS

Quantity 10 or 12 pansful. One quart flour; enough milk to make stiff batter; one-half teacup granulated sugar; one whole yeast cake; salt to taste; two eggs beaten together. Mix all ingredients together, dust with flour, cover with moist cloth and permit to stand for four hours. Add enough flour to make good stiff dough. Make small balls of them and put in pan sufficiently far apart so they will not touch in baking. Allow to rise, watch carefully and bake from 10 to 15 minutes.—*Mrs. W. H. Marsh, Calvert County.*

YULE CAKE BUNS

Make a sponge with 1 cup of yeast, 3 cups of milk, 1 cup of sugar and requisite quantity of flour. When light, add 2 cups of sugar, 2 eggs, 1 teaspoon of soda, nutmeg, and flour enough for a stiff batter; 1 cup of butter and lard. Rise again and when light roll out thick. Cut and place in pan. Bake when quite light. For the Yule cakes add raisins to taste, but not very many. *Mrs. T. Edward Hambleton, Baltimore County.*

WHOLE WHEAT SLOW WAFFLES

Three measuring cups of whole wheat flour (not sifted). One half cup of butter, three cups of milk, two eggs, one teaspoonful of salt, two *full* teaspoons baking powder. Mix flour, milk, salt, melted butter, beaten eggs, and baking powder last. Pour in greased (by lard) hot waffle irons, and cook over open *hot* fire— gas or coal, or on electric iron.

WHITE FLOUR WAFFLES

Same as above, using white in place of whole wheat flour and add one tablespoonful of granulated sugar.—*Mrs. Symington Dawson, (Mary Harris, Cook), Baltimore.*

CAKES AND PASTRIES

GLORIFIED GINGER BREAD

Four tablespoonsful of fat (butter or lard)—one-quarter cup maple syrup—one egg well beaten—one-half teaspoon salt—one-quarter teaspoon ginger—one-half cup sugar—one-quarter teaspoon cloves or allspice—one teaspoon cinnamon—one-half cup sour milk—one and one-half cups flour—five-eighths teaspoonful soda.

Beat liquid ingredients thoroughly, sift all the dry ingredients together and add to liquids. Beat until well mixed. Spread in a shallow pan. Sprinkle with cinnamon and a cupful of walnuts and bake in a slow oven about thirty-five minutes. When done cut in squares, serve with whipped cream to which a dash of cinnamon has been added.—*Miss Zaidee Browning, Garrett County.*

CAKE CHARLOTTE RUSSE

1 pint milk, 1 pint whipping cream, 1 egg, ½ cup sugar, 1 teaspoonful gelatine, 2 teaspoons vanilla, 1 pint stale sponge cake crumbs (not too fine) 10 English walnuts (broken). To make: Beat yolks of eggs. Put in same about half the sugar. Pour over this the milk, which must be boiled. Dissolve gelatine in two tablespoons cold water and pour the boiling mixture over it. Add rest of sugar and let cool. Beat egg white stiff. Whip cream. Add both to first mixture with the seasoning. Pour half in wet mold. Add cake crumbs and nuts to rest of mixture. Pour in wet mold. Chill for three or four hours. Turn out of mold. Garnish with maraschino cherries. Serves ten good helpings.—*Miss Marguerite Gray, Calvert County.*

ROSE HILL MANOR, FREDERICK COUNTY

("Rose Hill Manor," *just outside of Frederick, the residence of Thomas John-son, first State Governor of Maryland, is one of the most delightful spots in Maryland to lodge and dine.*

The Manor is a treat to visit, furnished throughout in the period of its hey-day, the early part of the Eighteenth Century, an atmosphere of hospitality and cozy welcome pervades. It would certainly be difficult to find a more charming place to dine or better food to enjoy.)

BLACK WALNUT CAKE

¾ lb. butter. 1 lb. sugar, 1 lb. flour, 1 nutmeg (ground), 6 eggs, ¾ lb. black walnuts. Bake in loaf.—*Mrs. Charles B. Trail, Frederick County.*

BROWNIES

2 squares of chocolate, 2 eggs, 1 cup sugar, 1 cup nuts, ½ cup melted butter, ½ cup of flour. Beat sugar into eggs, then the flour, melted butter, chocolate and nuts—bake twenty minutes in a hot oven.—*The Misses Reynolds, Rose Hill Manor Inn, Frederick County.*

BRIDE'S CAKE

¾ pound flour, one pound white sugar, 6 ounces nice butter and the whites of 14 eggs.—*Mrs. Robert Goldsborough Henry, Myrtle Grove, Talbot County.*

BUTTERLESS, EGGLESS, MILKLESS CAKE

Put in saucepan one cup brown sugar, two cups seeded raisins, scant one-half cup lard, one and one-half cups water, a pinch of salt, one teaspoonful cinnamon, one-quarter teaspoonful cloves, one-quarter teaspoonful nutmeg. Boil together three minutes, when cool, add one teaspoonful of baking soda dissolved in warm water, one teaspoonful of yeast powder sifted with two cups of flour. Mix and bake thirty-five minutes.—*Mrs. Dawson Orme George, Caroline County.*

CALIFORNIA CAKE

¼ lb. butter, 2 cups sugar, ¼ cup of milk, 1 pt. of sifted flour, 4 eggs, 2 teaspoonsful of cream of tartar, 1 teaspoonful of soda. Bake in a loaf.—*Mrs. Fanny E. Bratton, The Hermitage, Cecil County.*

WORKINGTON, SOMERSET COUNTY

CHOCOLATE CAKES

Whip the whites of six eggs to a stiff froth, add one pound of pulverized sugar and continue to beat for thirty minutes.

Stir in one-fifth of a pound of cocoa and one tablespoonful of vanilla extract.

Drop by teaspoonsful on greased pans and bake in a very moderate oven.—*Miss Elizabeth C. Remmert, Baltimore.*

BLACK CAKE

Three pounds butter, three pounds sugar, beaten, three glasses brandy, two glasses rose water, thirty eggs, three pounds flour, added by degrees, flour to be browned, six pounds currants, six pounds seeded raisins, one-half ounce cinnamon, three-fourths ounce nutmeg and mace, one-half ounce cloves, one pound citron, the peel of two oranges. Bake five hours if in one vessel. Almonds are a great improvement. If two pounds of almonds be added, reduce the quantity of currants and raisins one pound each. Two glasses of wine may be preferred to rose water (I substituted it). —*Mrs. Wm. Courtland Hart, Workington, Somerset County.*

COLUMBIA CAKE

1½ pounds of flour, 1 pound of sugar, ¾ pound of butter, 2 eggs, a little brandy and a little wine and a few currants.— *Receipt of the sisters, Sophonisba and Angelica Peale, daughters of Charles Willson Peale, preëminent artist of the era of the American Revolution.*

DOVER CAKE

One pound of flour, one pound of sugar, half a pound of butter, six eggs, half a nutmeg and a spoonful of rose brandy. Beat the butter and sugar together, adding the other ingredients, the whites of the eggs beaten separately. Bake as pound cake. (Rose brandy was merely the regular brandy into which rose leaves were allowed to soak.)—*Miss Julia Loker, Mulberry Fields, St. Mary's County.*

FRUIT CAKE

Cream one and one-half pounds of butter and one and one-half pounds of sugar, yolks of ten eggs, four wineglasses of milk, two wineglasses of brandy, two teaspoonsful of cinnamon, two teaspoonsful of baking powder, one salt spoonful of ground cloves, one teaspoonful allspice, two pounds of flour, adding one and one-half pounds to mixture and sprinkling the fruit with the other one-half pound. Add whites of eggs beaten stiff just before fruit. Two pounds of raisins, two pounds of currants, one pound of citron, two pounds of English walnuts, one pound of figs and one pound of dates.

Chop fruit fine and bake in a moderate oven for four hours. —*Mrs. Emerson C. Harrington, Jr., Dorchester County.*

FEDERAL CAKE

(1)

½ pound butter, the same of sugar, 1 pound of flour, a teaspoonful of cinnamon. Rub them all together with two eggs and a little rose water.

(2)

1 pound of flour, ½ pound of butter, the same of sugar, a little bit of cinnamon, 2 eggs. Wet it with water, make it into nice dough, roll it out thin and cut it with a teacup.—*Receipt of the sisters, Sophonisba and Angelica Peale, daughters of Charles Willson Peale, preëminent artist of the era of the American Revolution.*

DEVIL'S FOOD CAKE

White Part: 1½ cups granulated sugar, ½ cup butter, ½ cup sweet milk (little over), 1½ cups flour, 1 teaspoon baking powder, whites of 6 eggs.

Chocolate Part: 2/3 cup of granulated sugar, 2/3 cup grated chocolate, ½ cup of milk, yolk of 1 egg. Cook until thick, cool, add flavoring, then stir this in dough. (Bake in layers.)

Filling for outside: 2 cups brown sugar, 1 cup of cream, 2/3 cup grated chocolate, 2 tablespoons of butter, flavor with bitter almond. Cook until very thick, then take off and stir until cool, spread on cake.—*Mrs. A. M. Coffman, Prince George County.*

GINGER CAKES

(*Quantity: enough to last Dr. Marsh five nights*)

Two teacups molasses (Porto Rico molasses); one teacup sugar; two-thirds teacup of lard; one beaten egg stirred in it; two tablespoons ginger; one heaping tablespoonful bicarbonate of soda, salt to taste. Set on stove and let stew on a slow fire until everything is dissolved. Add flour enough to make it stiff enough to roll. Cut with cutter and bake.—*Mrs. W. H. Marsh, Calvert County.*

GOLD CAKE

One-half cupful butter, one-half cupful sugar, one-half cupful milk, two and one-half cupfuls flour, five eggs (all the yolks and one white), two teaspoonsful baking powder, two teaspoonsful vanilla.—*Miss Julia Loker, Mulberry Fields, St. Mary's County.*

COUNTRY CLUB INN

(AMONG *the pleasant and satisfying places to dine in Maryland is the Country Club Inn at Belair. It was originally the Eagle Hotel and was built in 1716. No antiques are sold, the purpose of the hostelry being today as it was well over a century ago to feed and lodge both man and beast. It is most attractively furnished and the atmosphere of a bygone day has been achieved with unstudied success.*)

GRAHAM CRACKER CAKE

20 ground graham crackers, 2 tablespoons flour, 1½ teaspoons baking powder, 1 cup sugar, scant half cup butter, ¾ cup sweet milk, 3 eggs (beaten separately) 1 cup chopped walnuts.

Cream the sugar and butter, add beaten egg yolks and milk. Mix the graham crackers and flour and baking powder together and add to the first mixture. Then add the walnuts and beaten egg whites last. Bake forty minutes at 350 degrees. When cold spread filling over the cake and serve with whipped cream.

Filling: One package dates, one cup sugar, one cup water. Boil until thick and spread on cake.—*J. Butterfield, Proprietor, The Country Club Inn, Harford County.*

216

MAHOGANY CAKE

2 squares of chocolate cut fine, 1 cup sugar, 1 egg well beaten, ½ cup coffee (cold), ½ cup fat, ½ cup sugar, 1 teaspoon vanilla, 2 eggs, ½ cup sour milk, ¼ teaspoon salt, 2½ cups flour, 1 teaspoon soda, 1 teaspoon baking powder.

Mix chocolate, one cup sugar and one egg with coffee. Cook slowly, stirring constantly until mixture thickens. Cool. Cream the ½ cup fat with the ½ cup sugar. Beat well the two eggs and add together with the vanilla and the sour milk. Beat two minutes. Add the cooled chocolate mixture, then the rest of the ingredients. Beat well and pour into two well-greased layer cake pans. Bake in slow oven, cool and frost with the following:

Creamy Nut Frosting: 2 cups brown sugar, 1 cup milk, ½ cup broken nuts, 1 tablespoon vanilla, 1 tablespoon butter. Mix sugar, milk and butter, cook slowly, stirring constantly, until a soft ball forms when a portion is tried in cold water. Cool fifteen minutes. Beat until creamy, add nuts and frost cake.—*Mrs. J. H. Windsor, Windsor Manor, Baltimore County.*

LADY BALTIMORE CAKE

One cup of butter, two cups of sugar, one cup of milk, three and a half cups of flour, two teaspoons of baking powder, one teaspoon of rose water.

Add the whites of six eggs. Bake in three layers in hot oven.

In the icing add a cup of raisins and nuts (pecans preferred), and about five figs cut fine or in thin strips.—*Mrs. William T. Delaplaine, Frederick County.*

JELLY CAKE

Sift three-quarters of a pound of flour. Stir to a cream, one pound of butter, one pound of powdered white sugar and mix in half a teacup of rose water and a grated nutmeg. Beat ten eggs very light, alternately with the flour, stirring the whole very hard. Put your griddle into the oven of the stove and when it is quite hot grease it with a little butter tied in a clean rag and set on it a tin cake ring. Dip out two and a half tablespoonsful of the batter and bake it about five minutes. When the cakes are cold spread every one very thickly with grape jelly. Lay the cakes smoothly one on another. Either grate loaf sugar on the top one or ice it smoothly.—*Miss Julia Loker, Mulberry Fields, St. Mary's County.*

LEMON CHEESE CAKES

One-half pound butter, one-half pound loaf sugar, eight eggs beat very fine, four of the whites left out, rind of one lemon grated, two teaspoonsful of the juice; simmer them together until they turn rather thick, put it in a rich paste (pastry or pie crust); bake it in small pans.—*Miss Rebecca Hollingsworth French, Washington County.*

POUND CAKE

One pound of sugar, one pound of butter, a light pound of flour, nine eggs, one teaspoonful of soda. Season with brandy and nutmeg.—*Mrs. Natalie J. Digges, Charles County.*

OLD-FASHIONED CUP CAKE

Four cups of flour, three cups of sugar, one cup butter, one cup sour milk, one scant teaspoon soda thoroughly mixed with the milk, six eggs.

Cream butter and sugar together; beat the yolks and whites of eggs separately; flavor with lemon. Use fruit and spices if you like. Excellent for layer or patty cakes.—*J. Butterfield, Proprietor, The Country Club Inn, Harford County.*

MOLASSES CAKE

1 cup New Orleans molasses, 1 cup brown sugar, ¼ lb. butter, 1 cup sour milk or cream, 2 eggs, 4 cups flour, 2 teaspoons soda (even ones) dissolved in hot water and added to the molasses, 2 teaspoons ginger, 1 teaspoon cinnamon, juice and rind of one orange. Bake in slow oven as molasses burns quickly; test with straw; if it does not stick to it, it is done.—*Mrs. Nora D. Bratten, Worcester County.*

"NONE SO GOOD"

(*Plain Cakes*)

Half pound of butter, one pound of sugar, three eggs, one and one-half cups of milk, one teaspoonful each of lemon and vanilla. One pound of flour. One teaspoonful of baking powder. —*Miss Kittie S. Quynn, of Frederick, niece of Miss Emily E. Hanshew, who was grandniece of Barbara Fritchie, the heroine of Whittier's poem.*

WASHINGTON, AFTER CHARLES WILLSON PEALE

CHEESE STRAWS

1 cup cheese grated very fine, 1 cup butter, dash of red pepper, 1 cup sifted flour, just enough cold water to mix as in pie crust. Roll thin, fold twice, rolling each time. Cut in long thin strips. Place in a pan without touching and bake a very light brown.—*Mrs. Irving Adams, Howard County.*

WASHINGTON CAKE

1¾ pounds of superfine flour, 1¾ pounds of brown sugar, ¾ pound of butter, 8 eggs, 1 pound of Sultana raisins, 1 pound of currants, 2 wineglasses of brandy, 1 pint of milk or cream, a little rose water. Spice to suit the taste, with a teaspoonful of Pearlash in the rose water or brandy. Butter paper and put in 2 pans and bake 3 hours.—*Receipt of the sisters, Sophonisba and Angelica Peale, daughters of Charles Willson Peale, preëminent artist of the era of the American Revolution.*

SPONGE CAKE

(*To be iced with orange icing*)

4 eggs beaten together, 2 cups granulated sugar, 2 cups flour, ¾ cup boiling water, stir in slowly, juice of 1 lemon, 1 heaping teaspoon of yeast powder. Bake in layers in a good oven. (This will make three layers.)

Orange Icing

2 cups of granulated sugar, ½ cup cold water, whites of 2 eggs, grated rind of 1 orange, and cut the 1 orange in very thin small pieces. Boil the sugar and water until it strings from spoon, pour this over the beaten whites of 2 eggs, stir in the grated rind of orange, and put small pieces of orange on layer of cake, then put on the icing. Do not put the small pieces of orange on the top layer. Put only the icing on the last layer. (This will spread one three-layer cake.)—*Mrs. George Wilson, Prince George County.*

SPONGE CAKE

Weight of ten eggs in sugar, weight of six eggs in flour, whites of twelve eggs, yolks of nine eggs, grated rind and juice of one lemon. Beat yolks very light, add sugar and lemon and beat again. Beat whites until very stiff and add, then beat all together fifteen minutes, add flour, stirring as little as possible.

Lemon Filling: 1 lemon grated rind and pulp, 2 eggs, 6 oz. granulated sugar, lump butter size of an egg. Put all in double boiler and cook until it thickens, stirring frequently.—*Mrs. Victor Miller, Washington County.*

SPICE CAKES

1 egg, 1½ cups flour, 2 teaspoons baking powder, 1 cup sugar, ½ cup water, 1 cup raisins, 1 large tablespoon cinnamon, ½ tablespoon cloves, juice and grated rind of 1 lemon, butter size of an egg. Cream butter and sugar, add yolk of egg well beaten, then the white beaten stiff, add water and flour; lastly add spices and raisins.—*Mrs. Bernard Freeman, Baltimore.*

MARBLE CAKE

Take one-half cup of butter and beat well with one and a half cups of powdered sugar. Add the whites of four eggs well beaten to a stiff froth, one-half cup of milk, two and a half cups of flour, and two and a half teaspoonsful of baking powder. Flavor to taste and bake.—*Miss Julia Loker, Mulberry Fields, St. Mary's County.*

WHITE FRUIT CAKE

2 cups sugar, 1 cup butter, 1 cup milk, 2½ cups flour, ¼ lb. citron, whites of seven eggs, 2 teaspoons baking powder, 1 cocoanut grated, 1 lb. almonds blanched and chopped, ½ lb. conserved cherries, ½ teaspoon salt. Flavor with bitter almond.

Sift flour, salt and baking powder three times; cream shortening and sugar. Add egg whites one at a time, beating well after each is added. Add bitter almond and milk with flour alternately, a little at a time. Mix citron, cocoanut, almonds and cherries together and sift a *little* of the 2½ cups of flour through them—keeps fruit from settling at bottom of pan. Bake in greased loaf pan in moderate oven *1 hour* or more if necessary.—*Mrs. Nora D. Bratten, Worcester County.*

ICE BOX COOKIES

Cream one-half cup butter, add gradually one cup light brown sugar, then one egg well beaten. One and three-quarter cups bread flour mixed with one-half teaspoonful soda and one-quarter teaspoonful salt, one-half cup chopped nut meats. This mixture is without liquid, is very stiff and should be packed solidly into a well-buttered bread pan.

Leave in ice box overnight.

When ready to bake turn from mold. Slice as thinly as possible and bake on buttered pans.

This makes three dozen cookies.—*Miss Mary McDaniel, Talbot County.*

MAPLE SYRUP COOKIES

One cup of butter, three large eggs, one and one-half cups maple syrup, three cups flour, one teaspoon baking powder, one teaspoonful soda dissolved in one-half cup of hot water, one cup of black walnut meats, one and one-half cups of dates cut in pieces. Mix well. Drop by spoonfuls on a pan and bake in moderate oven. Cook slowly.—*Miss Zaidee Browning, Garrett County.*

OATMEAL COOKIES

2 eggs, 1 cup sugar, ¾ cup butter and lard, equal quantities, 2 cups flour with heaping teaspoonful cinnamon sifted in, a pinch of salt, 1 teaspoonful soda dissolved in tablespoonful hot water, 3 tablespoonfuls sweet milk, 1 cup chopped raisins, 2 cups dry oatmeal. Mix in order named and drop from spoon on buttered pan.—*Miss Mary W. Crisfield, Somerset County.*

SPICE COOKIES

Beat 4 eggs (whites and yolks) with 1 pound of brown sugar, add 1 pound of flour into which have been sifted 3 teaspoonfuls of cinnamon, 1 of allspice, 1 of cloves, 1 of baking powder, some grated nutmeg and the grated rind of a lemon. Mix well, add flour sufficient to roll out, cut into squares and bake in a moderate oven. For icing use juice of lemon stiffened with pulverized sugar.—*Miss Elizabeth C. Remmert, Baltimore.*

SUGAR COOKIES

½ pound butter, ½ pound lard, 2 ounces lemon extract, 1 pound granulated sugar, 6 eggs, flour sufficient to make soft dough.

Cream shortening and sugar. Add unbeaten eggs. Add flavoring and flour. Chill dough and take small amount at a time and roll out very thin. Cut in fancy shapes and bake to a light golden brown.—*Mrs. J. H. Windsor, Windsor Manor, Baltimore County.*

CRULLERS

One pint of milk, one pint of sugar, one-quarter pound of butter, three eggs, one teaspoonful of soda, two teaspoonfuls of cream of tartar, sift in enough flour to roll out. Flavor with lemon and fry in lard. Roll in sifted sugar and cinnamon when baked.—*Dr. Walter Forman Wickes, Wickcliffe, Greenspring Valley, Baltimore County.*

MARYLAND DOUGHNUTS

Two eggs, one-half a cup of sugar, two tablespoons butter, one-half a cup of milk, one teaspoon of yeast powder, one-quarter teaspoon of salt, one-quarter teaspoon nutmeg, one and one-half cups of flour, add more flour if needed. Cream the butter, sugar and eggs together. Add milk, flour and dry ingredients. Put on flour board and roll out one-half inch thick, cut with a cutter with a hole in the middle, fry in deep fat, as it begins to smoke. —*Mrs. James H. Preston, Baltimore.*

SOTTERLEY

(THESE *receipts from "Sotterley," St. Mary's County, were contributed through the courtesy of Mrs. James H. Parran, whose mother, Jeanette Briscoe, from whom these receipts were handed down, was born at "Sotterley." They originated with Mrs. Parran's grandmother, Mrs. W. H. S. Briscoe. "Sotterley" was built by George Plater in 1730, who left it upon his death to his son who was later destined to become Governor of Maryland. Later the grandson of the Governor also bearing his name lost the estate over the gaming table to Colonel Somerville, the builder and original owner of "Mulberry Fields." Somerville later sold it to Colonel Thomas Barber, whose adopted daughter married Dr. W. H. S. Briscoe, grandfather of Mrs. James B. Parran. "Sotterley" is owned at present by the Hon. Herbert L. Satterlee, son-in-law of the late Pierpont Morgan.*)

JUMBLES

One quart of flour, one point of sugar, one-quarter pound of butter, one-quarter pound of lard, four eggs, one nutmeg, one wineglass of brandy, one teaspoonful soda. Mix together the eggs, butter and seasoning and pour on the flour, beat light, roll in sheet and bake.—*Mrs. Natalie J. Digges, Charles County.*

226

JUMBLES

Three pounds of flour, two pounds of sugar, one pound of butter, six eggs, one cup of milk, one teaspoon of yeast powder. Sprinkle nutmeg and cinnamon through the flour. Cream the sugar and butter and pour on the well-beaten eggs, and then work in the flour. Pinch off small pieces of the dough and roll in sugar, nutmeg and cinnamon, give the ends a twist or tie. Bake in biscuit pan in moderate oven about fifteen minutes.— *Mrs. James B. Parran, Sotterley, St. Mary's County.*

SAND TARTS

2 lbs. flour, 2 lbs. sugar, 1 lb. butter, 3 eggs, ¾ lb. almonds. Knead thoroughly. Roll very thin. Cut in squares or round. Brush with white of egg. Sift sugar and cinnamon over each cake. Put an almond in center of each. Bake in quick oven.— *Mrs. Charles B. Trail, Frederick County.*

LEMON PIES

6 eggs, 4 lemons (juice), 1 pound sugar, 1 tablespoon flour, 1 glass sherry, 1 nutmeg, ½ pound butter. Cream butter and sugar and add the lemon, nutmeg and sherry. Add this to the beaten yolks of six eggs and add beaten egg whites and flour. Place this in pastry and bake in a moderate oven. (This should make two large or three small pies.)—*Mrs. Thomas Nalle Magruder, Prince George County.*

LEMON PUDDING

(*A pie*)

Juice of two lemons, rind of one, half pound of butter, four eggs, glass of wine, half cup of cream. Sweeten to your taste, and bake on pastry.—*Miss Amelia H. Birnie, Carroll County.*

COCONUT JUMBLES

½ lb. butter, ¾ lb. flour sifted, 3 eggs, 1 large coconut, save milk and use if necessary (if dough becomes too stiff), 1 lb. white sugar. Mix butter and sugar; add eggs, flour and grated coconut. Mix well and drop in small lumps into pan, bake quickly.—*Mrs. Victor Miller, Washington County.*

WALNUT MACAROONS

Whip the whites of six eggs to a stiff froth, add one pound of pulverized sugar and continue to beat for thirty minutes.

Stir in one pound of black walnuts (cut up very fine), drop by teaspoonfuls on paper spread on baking pans and bake in a very moderate oven.—*Miss Elizabeth C. Remmert, Baltimore.*

CARAMEL PIE

One cup of butter, one cup of sugar, four eggs, one cup of damson or plum preserve, one teaspoonful vanilla. Take seeds out of preserves and chop fine. Bake in pastry.—*Mrs. Natalie J. Digges, Charles County.*

"*Who touches a hair of yon grey head*
Dies like a dog! March on!" *he said.*—John Greenleaf Whittier.

COCONUT JUMBLES

Half a pound of butter, one pound of sugar, four **eggs**, **two** coconuts grated, three-quarters of a pound of flour.—*Miss Kittie S. Quynn of Frederick, niece of Miss Emily E. Hanshew, who was the grandniece of Barbara Fritchie, the heroine of Whittier's poem.*

229

MINCE MEAT

Twelve pounds lean meat boiled down to six pounds; six pounds suet, meat and suet put through meat chopper; six pounds of raisins; six pounds currants; one peck of apples chopped fine; five pounds brown sugar; three tablespoonsful ground cloves; two teaspoonsful ground mace; three tablespoonsful ground allspice; two tablespoonsful powdered nutmeg; salt to taste; one-half pound citron, cut fine. Mix thoroughly and "moisten" with one gallon of pre-war whisky. Pack in stone crocks until ready for use. When making pies, thin down to a proper consistency with either cider, rum or whisky, preferably Jamaica rum.—*Mrs. W. H. Marsh, Calvert County.*

MINCE MEAT

1 lb. lean beef chopped fine, 1½ lb. raisins, 2 lbs. currants washed and dried, 8 pippin apples pared and chopped, 2 lbs. suet chopped fine, 1 lb. citron sliced thin, 2 lemons grated, the juice of ½ of one, 2 lbs. brown sugar, 2 nutmegs, 1 teaspoon powdered mace, 1 pinch powdered cloves, 1 quart wine, 1 pint brandy or rum.

These measurements are for the ingredients after they are prepared, i.e., after the beef is cooked, chopped and all the fat or gristle removed, it must weigh one pound.

This will make fifteen pies.

Put in a stone jar, tie up tightly, and it will keep several weeks in a cool place. The mince meat should be very moist; it may therefore be necessary to add a little more wine.—*Mrs. E. Glenn Perine, Baltimore.*

ORANGE PIE

Two measuring cups of water, one cup orange juice; cut rind in very fine thin slivers using about one half teaspoonful; three-quarters cup sugar, two tablespoons corn starch, one tablespoon flour. For meringue use two tablespoons of sugar to two eggs.—*Mrs. Dawson Orme George, Caroline County.*

SHOO FLY PIE

One cup molasses, one cup boiling water with one teaspoon baking soda, one cup sugar, one cup flour, butter size of an egg.

Mix water, molasses and soda. Pour into pie crust, mix sugar, flour and butter into crumbs. Put on top of pie. Season with cinnamon if liked.

Makes one pie.—*Mrs. George H. Birnie, Carroll County.*

SWEET POTATO PIE

2 good-sized sweet potatoes, 3 eggs, butter the size of a walnut, 1 cup of milk, ½ cup sugar, 1 teaspoonful cinnamon. Wash potatoes and parboil them. When quite cool peel and grate them. Beat the butter, sugar and yolks of eggs until very light. Add potatoes by degrees, stirring all the while, then add other ingredients. Line a deep pie dish with pastry, fill it with this mixture, and bake half an hour. Then beat the whites of the eggs to a stiff froth with 2 tablespoons of sugar. Heap over the pie and brown in oven. Serve in pie dish. Serve cold.—*Mrs. Charles B. Trail, Frederick County.*

PUMPKIN PIE

1½ cups cooked pumpkin, ¾ cup brown sugar, ½ cup milk, ¼ cup cream, 2 eggs, ½ teaspoonful cinnamon, ½ teaspoonful nutmeg, ¼ teaspoonful salt, filling for one pie crust.—*Mrs. W. T. Hamilton, Washington County.*

TYLER PUDDING PIE

(TYLER PUDDING PIE *was named in honor of John Tyler, tenth President of the United States. This receipt was handed down in the Clary family, of Claryville, Allegany County, Maryland.*)

One and a half cups of brown sugar, one and a half cups of white sugar, one cup of butter, one cup of cream, five eggs, vanilla, and nutmeg.

Melt the butter and cream in a double boiler. Beat the eggs until very light. Then pour in the butter and cream mixture. Add vanilla. Pour into uncooked pie crust, and dust with nutmeg. Bake in a very slow oven until very brown. Makes two pies.—*Mrs. George S. Rodock, Frederick County.*

JELLIES, PRESERVES, AND PICKLES

CHIEF JUSTICE ROGER BROOKE TANEY

(CHIEF JUSTICE ROGER BROOKE TANEY, *one of the most picturesque figures in American history, swore into office more Presidents—seven in all—than any other Chief Justice. He was the author of the famous Dred Scott decision.*)

CALF'S FEET JELLY

To a set of feet put two gallons of water. Boil it down to one. Set it away to cool. Skim it. Put it in a skillet. Season it to your taste with lemon juice, sugar and wine. Throw in the rind. Clarify it with the whites and shells of six eggs. Then strain through a flannel bag until clean.

This receipt shows that the Maryland housewives and their negro slaves knew how to make calf's feet jelly clear, as they did in England, with the use of "the whites and shells of eggs." A voluminous old English cook book says: "We hear inexperienced housekeepers frequently complain of the difficulty of rendering this jelly perfectly transparent; but by mixing with the other ingredients, while quite cold, the whites, and the crushed shells of a sufficient number of eggs, and by allowing the head of scum which gathers on the jelly to remain undisturbed after it once forms, they will scarcely fail to obtain it clear. It should be strained through a thick flannel, or beaver-skin bag, of conical form (placed before the fire, should the weather be at all cold, or the mixture will jell before it has run through), and if not perfectly clear it must be strained, again and again, until it becomes so; though we generally find that once suffices."—*The Misses Lelia and Alice Taney, Frederick County.*

SPICED CANTALOUPE

Take ripe cantaloupe, slice, pare and pack in jar, cover with vinegar and let stand overnight. Pour off vinegar; to every quart add 2½ lbs. of sugar, cloves and cinnamon and mace to taste (all whole).

Put vinegar, sugar and spices on to boil, add fruit and boil 40 minutes; when fruit is clear remove from syrup, then boil syrup a little longer, replacing fruit for a few minutes—not over ten—take from fire and put in jars.—*Mrs. Irving Adams, Howard County.*

BAR-LE-DUC

Two quarts gooseberries, one quart currants, eight cups sugar. Mash gooseberries well, add one-half pint water and cook one-half hour. Add sugar and cook one-half hour. Add currants and cook until it jells.—*Miss Mary McDaniel, Talbot County.*

APPLE JELLY

Take some apples, wipe and cut them up without paring or coring. Boil them in water enough to cover them. Boil them until very soft. Put them in a coarse bag to drip. Add one pound sugar to one pint of syrup, the juice of one lemon to every quart of syrup. Boil syrup and sugar one-half hour, skimming occasionally.—*Mrs. J. Morsell Roberts, Calvert County.*

CALVES' FOOT JELLY

Boil 4 calves' feet, making 2 quarts jelly. When cold strain off the grease, then pour into it 1 quart white wine, juice of 6 lemons (strained), 1½ pounds sugar, cinnamon, mace, the rind of 2 lemons. Whip the whites of 8 eggs to a froth, crush the shells and mix with the jelly. Strain.—*Mrs. E. Glenn Perine, Baltimore.*

CRANBERRY JELLY

One quart of berries, one-half pint of water. Boil ten minutes. Strain, add half pound sugar, boil twenty minutes.—*Miss Louisa Ogle Thomas, Baltimore.*

NORTHAMPTON MANOR

(*Destroyed by fire 1909*)

("NORTHAMPTON" *was the Maryland home of the distinguished family of Fair-faxes. The original grant of land was by Lord Baltimore in 1650 and is reputed to have been laid out by L'Enfant, who made the city plans of our National Capital. In 1869 John Contee Fairfax, who lived at Northampton Manor for many years, received the title of eleventh Baron Fairfax of Cameron and as such his right to a seat in the English House of Lords.*)

CURRANT JELLY

The currants should be picked from the bushes during dry weather. Place the currants over the fire in an agate or porcelain-lined kettle, having first crushed them very slightly to draw out enough juice to keep them from burning. As soon as they are cooked soft, strain through a fine crash bag until all the juice is extracted, then strain it slowly through a flannel jelly-bag to remove all impurities and pulp. Measure the juice and put it in a clean kettle. For every pound of juice allow one pound of granulated sugar. Put the sugar in a stone crock large enough to hold the juice. Let the juice boil hard for five minutes, then pour it over the sugar in the jar, stirring all the time and until the sugar is dissolved. Dip it immediately into the tumblers. It will often be solid jelly before it is cold.—*Mrs. Clarence J. Roberts, née Miss Frances Fairfax, Prince George's County.*

GRAPE CONSERVE

Five pounds grapes, four pounds sugar, two oranges with some grated rind, one pound English walnut meats, one pound raisins.

Pulp the grapes and cook ten minutes. Press through a colander. Add skins and sugar, juice and pulp, raisins and nuts.

Cook twenty minutes.—*Mrs. George H. Birnie, Carroll County.*

CUCUMBER CATSUP

Grate on bread grater 1/3 as many onions as fully grown cucumbers, drain off some of the cucumber juice, but none of the onion. To every quart of cucumber and onion juice add 1½ pints strong vinegar. To each gallon of juice (cucumber, onion and vinegar) put 1 cup brown sugar, 2 tablespoons of salt, 2 tablespoons of mustard and 3 tablespoons of black pepper. Put in bottle and cork tight.—*Mrs. Caleb Clarke Magruder, Prince George County.*

CHILI SAUCE

Pare 12 large tomatoes and chop fine, two large onions chopped fine, 4 medium-sized green peppers. Cut vegetables separately and stir all together and add as follows:

2 tablespoonsful salt, 2 tablespoonsful sugar, 1 tablespoonful cinnamon, 3 teacups of vinegar.

Boil one and one-half hours, stirring well, and bottle as catsup.—*Mrs. J. Morsell Roberts, Calvert County.*

PICKLED CANTALOUPE

To six pounds of rind take four of sugar, make a rich syrup with vinegar enough to cover the fruit, boil and skim, add spices for taste, such as ginger, mustard seed, cloves, mace, whole grains of black pepper, horse-radish cut in chips.

Before putting the fruit in the syrup, boil in weak alum water fifteen minutes. Drain well and boil in the syrup until clear, which will be one or two hours.—*Dr. Walter Forman Wickes, Wickcliffe, Greenspring Valley, Baltimore County.*

CHERRY PRESERVES

Wash and seed the cherries. To two cups of cherries add two level cups of sugar. Put over slow fire until the sugar is melted. Gradually increase the heat and cook until the syrup is thick. Pour into glasses.

Prepare only two cups of fruit at a time, as this prevents the cherries from turning dark.—*Mr. J. F. Essary, Baltimore.*

CHOW CHOW

One peck green tomatoes, one quarter peck onions, one dozen green peppers (sweet), one head of cabbage, one dozen medium size cucumbers, five cents' worth of mustard seed, three pounds brown sugar, cut all up and put in bin overnight. Drain next morning and cover well with vinegar. Cook slowly until done.—*Mrs. Eloise Hance, Calvert County.*

SPICED GRAPES

5 pounds of grapes, 3 pounds of sugar, 2 teaspoonsful cinnamon, 2 teaspoonsful allspice, ½ teaspoonful cloves. Pulp grapes, boil skins until tender. Cook pulp and strain through a sieve; add all ingredients, add vinegar to taste and boil thoroughly. Place in jars and seal.—*Mrs. Alexander D. Toadvin, Wicomico County.*

ISINGLASS JELLY

Use two ounces at least of isinglass, which should be first soaked in cold water for two hours. Drain off that water, then take two quarts of boiling water, one and one-half pounds of sugar, a pint of wine, all according to your taste, the juice of three good-sized lemons; peel off one, then beat the whites of four eggs, mix all well together before putting it on the fire; boil it twenty minutes. Do not stir the jelly after the froth collects. Before taking it off the fire, pour in a wineglass of cold water and skim some of the froth off before putting it in the strainer. If you wish to mold it, use four ounces of isinglass instead of two. —*Miss Rebecca Hollingsworth French, Washington County.*

ISINGLASS JELLY

To one ounce of shaved isinglass put one quart of water. Boil it to a pint and strain it through a flannel bag. Add sugar, wine and lemon to your taste.—*Mrs. William Courtland Hart, Somerset County.*

(ISINGLASS *is a firm, whitish, semi-transparent substance, being a comparatively pure form of gelatine obtained from the sounds or air-bladders of some fresh-water fishes, especially the sturgeon. It is used in cookery for making jelly and also for clarifying liquors, and in the manufacture of glue as well as for other purposes. This definition dates from the year 1545 to the present time.*
Also, a name given to mica because it resembles in appearance some type of isinglass. It came into use in 1747.)

STUFFED MANGOES

The mangoes are put in brine (hot) to remain a week. Then place them in vinegar to remain two weeks. At the end of that time, cut open the side and remove the seed. For stuffing use the following articles:

White mustard seed, mace pounded, celery seed, scraped horse-radish, and one clove of garlic to each mango.—*Mrs. Wm. D. Poultney, Baltimore.*

CANDIED GRAPE FRUIT RIND

Put grape fruit rind in salt and water overnight. Cut in strips and measure. Put in cold water and boil for twenty minutes. Do this three times; same amount of sugar as fruit and very little water; boil for half an hour or a little longer, till perfectly tender. Drain syrup off and dip strips of fruit in sugar and lay on cloth till cold. Leave open.—*Mrs. Wm. H. Thomas, Carroll County.*

BELAIR

(SAMUEL OGLE, *the great-great-great-grandfather of Louisa Ogle Thomas, came to Maryland as Governor in 1737. He married the daughter of Governor Tasker, who owned "Belair." The Ogle family is one of the most ancient and aristocratic families of England, dating back before the time of William the Conqueror. It was Governor Ogle who imported race horses from England and first introduced this picturesque and atmospheric sport into the State of Maryland.*)

BRANDIED PEACHES

Have ready a strong lye, boiling, throw your peaches in it and let them stand a few minutes, then with a coarse towel wipe the fur off, and then put them in cold water, take them through several waters (all cold) until no slippery feeling is left upon them, then weigh them and put them in a closed vessel with ½ pound sugar to 1 pound of peaches, cover them with water and then cover them close in your vessel, boil them briskly until you can pass a straw through them, pour the syrup and all in a closed vessel and set them away until cold, then pour the syrup off and put it to boil, stew it one-half away, measure it and add as much brandy as syrup, then pour it over the peaches and set them away for use. (Do not put too many peaches in the lye at one time as they spoil to remain in any length of time.)—*Mrs. Mordecai Plummer, Prince George's County.*

CHOP PICKLE

Two heads of cabbage, six yellow cucumbers, twelve onions, four green peppers. Put cucumbers in brine two days, peel off the skin and cut in cubes, put in fresh water one night. Cut cabbage, onions and peppers and sprinkle with salt overnight, and thoroughly wash in morning. Put in kettle with the following spices: two pounds of sugar, two ounces mustard seed, one ounce celery seed, one small box mustard, one ounce turmeric, cover over with vinegar and boil thirty minutes.—*Mr. and Mrs. J. Spence Howard, St. Mary's Manor, St. Mary's County.*

SPICED PEACHES

5 lbs, peaches. 3 lbs. sugar, ½ pt. *cider* vinegar, scant tablespoon whole allspice, scant tablespoon whole cloves, scant tablespoon cinnamon bark.

Tie spices in a thin cloth and crush them. This is only to flavor them, do not put the bag or spices in jars with fruit. Boil all ingredients together. When peaches are tender remove them until syrup cooks the proper consistency, return peaches to the syrup and set away to cool. Put in air-tight pint jars.

Above receipt fills four or five pints.—*Mrs. Frederick P. Stieff, Sr., Baltimore.*

GINGER PEAR

7 lbs. of fruit sliced thin in small pieces, 6 lbs. sugar, juice and rind of three lemons, ½ lb. of preserved ginger.—*The Misses Reynolds, Rose Hill Manor Inn, Frederick County.*

CHOW CHOW PICKLE

25 green cucumbers, 2 large heads of cabbage, 15 onions, salt overnight, next day squeeze very dry by wringing through a cloth, put all into half vinegar and water for three days. Drain very dry again, add 1 pint grated horse-radish, ½ pound white mustard seed, 1 ounce celery seed, ½ teacup of ground black pepper, 2 boxes mustard, 1½ ounces of turmeric, 1 pound of brown sugar. Boil pure vinegar and pour over it; do this for three days; at each boiling add a little more vinegar.—*Miss Mary E. Clagett, Prince George's County.*

MUSHROOM CATSUP

Take a bushel of the large mushrooms gathered dry, bruise them with your hands. Put some in an earthen pan, strew some salt over them, then mushrooms, then salt, then mushrooms till done. Put in one-half ounce of beaten cloves and mace, the same of allspice and let them stand a day or two. Stir them up every day, then put them in a stew pan and boil them. When done strain them through a cloth to get all the liquor out and let it stand to settle. Pour it off clear from the settlings. It must be boiled until one-third reduced. Strain it through a sieve into a pan. Pour it from the settlings and bottle for use. Cork tightly.—*Mrs. Wm. D. Poultney, Baltimore.*

CHERRY PICKLE

10 pounds cherries, 1 quart vinegar, 4 pounds brown sugar, a few spices. Boil until fruit is tender.—*Mrs. Robert Lee Hall, Prince George's County.*

PINEAPPLE MARMALADE OR JAM

Pare and grate the pineapples to pulp and juice, on a coarse tin rasp, or grater. Weigh it, and to one pound of the pulp put three-quarter pound of sugar, boil it gently to the consistency of raspberry jam.—*Miss Rebecca Hollingsworth French, Washington County.*

PICCALILLI

(THE *historic old mansion "Rose Hill" was built in 1801 by Captain David Lynn, progenitor of the Lynn family in the State of Maryland.*

It overlooks the Potomac River with a beautiful view into West Virginia and the mountains of Maryland that surround the city of Cumberland.

It was purchased and restored in 1904 by Col. John Williams Avirett, owner and editor of the "Evening Times" for thirty years, whose death oc-curred in 1914.

Mrs. Avirett later married the late Dr. James Walter Thomas, lawyer and historian.

The mansion has entertained many prominent people and Mrs. Avirett Thomas still dispenses delightful hospitality.)

2 dozen green tomatoes, 2 dozen large cucumbers, 1 dozen small cucumbers, 1 dozen onions, 1 cabbage, 6 bunches celery, 6 large green peppers. Chop, mix, stir in a handful of salt. Let it stand 2 hours and then put in a colander to drain. Pour 1 quart water and 2 quarts vinegar into a porcelain kettle and when it boils put into the mixture, a part at a time, and scald 10 minutes.

Skim and drain again, place in small jars and pour in the following, scalding hot: 1 gallon vinegar, 3 pounds sugar, ½ pound white mustard seed, 2 tablespoons ground mustard, 1 tablespoon black pepper, 3 tablespoons cinnamon, 1 tablespoon cloves, 1 teaspoon cayenne pepper.—*Mrs. Sarah D. Avirett Thomas, Allegany County.*

PEPPER RELISH

One dozen large sweet peppers (six red, three yellow, three green), one medium head of cabbage, four large onions, one pound of white sugar, one quart of vinegar, one heaping tablespoonful of celery seed, one heaping tablespoon of ground mustard, a little black pepper.

Grind cabbage and onions in meat chopper, cover with salt and let stand several hours or overnight and drain well. Grind peppers and add to other vegetables. Bring to a boil the vinegar, sugar and spices and when cool pour over the vegetables. Do not put in airtight jars. It is ready for immediate use and will keep.
—*Miss Rebecca Hollingsworth French, Washington County.*

GREEN TOMATO PICKLE

Wash and cut up 1 peck green tomatoes, slice thin 2 quarts white onions, put in stone jar and salt, let stand overnight. The next day turn in a colander and drain. Put in porcelain kettle with 1 quart vinegar and 1 quart water and cook over moderate fire. Allow tomatoes and onions to simmer until clear and tender. Again turn in colander and drain. Put 2 quarts vinegar in kettle with 2 lbs. brown sugar, ½ lb. of white mustard seed, 1 tablespoon each of ground pepper, allspice, cloves, celery seed. Heat slowly to a boil. Meanwhile mix together a teaspoon of turmeric, ½ teaspoon cayenne pepper, and ½ teaspoon ground mustard. Stir into the vinegar and pour over the pickle. Mix carefully with a wooden spoon. Lastly, add 1 teacup of best salad oil. Set aside until cool, then put in jars or crocks.—*Mrs. Charles B. Trail, Frederick County.*

MUSTARD PICKLE

Cut 2 quarts green tomatoes, 2 heads of cauliflower, 4 green peppers, 2 dozen small cucumbers, 1 quart of small onions. Let stand in brine overnight. In morning scald, but do not boil, then drain brine. Mix 1 cup flour and 6 tablespoons mustard, 1 tablespoon turmeric in cold vinegar. Let 2 cups vinegar and 2 cups sugar come to a boil, add flour and mustard, add pickle mixture and scald slowly. (Only use 4 tablespoons mustard if you use Coleman's.)—*Mrs. Harry W. Gore, Prince George's County.*

RED TOMATO PICKLE

One peck ripe tomatoes, stick them with fork and put them in brine for eight days. Then soak in clear water for an hour. Cut ten onions in slices and lay in salt water for one hour, drain and add to tomatoes.

Add one ounce of whole cloves, one ounce of allspice, one ounce of black pepper, one ounce of mustard.—*Mr. and Mrs. George R. Dennis, Mt. Hampton, Frederick County.*

PRESERVING WHOLE ORANGES

Peel them, and let soak in cold water for an hour, then boil until you can stick a straw in them, make a hole in the top, and with a penknife take out the seeds, make a syrup of one pound of sugar to a pound of fruit, boil until clear, put oranges in syrup and boil a few minutes, skim syrup if necessary. (Only take the yellow part of peel off.)—*Mrs. Mordecai Plummer, Prince George's County.*

GERMAN PICKLE

Four pounds of fruit wiped dry and add one ounce of cinnamon, one ounce of cloves. Put a layer of each in a stone jar, then boil one quart of sharp vinegar with three pounds of brown sugar. Skim it and pour it boiling hot over the fruit. Let them stand twenty-four hours, pour the juice off, then boil it again and pour it over the fruit. After they stand another twenty-four hours boil the whole, just scalding the fruit. When quite cold put them into the jars and cover the fruit with the syrup. Bind them over with a bladder and set them in a cool place.—*Miss Rebecca Hollingsworth French, Washington County.*

COLD RELISH

Take three medium-sized carrots, two heads of cabbage, eight medium-sized onions, nine red sweet peppers, nine green peppers, one-half cup salt, three pints of vinegar, two pints of sugar, two tablespoons of white mustard seeds and two tablespoons of celery seeds.

Grind the scraped carrots, the peeled onions and the seeded peppers. Chop the cabbage right fine. (Grinding the cabbage makes it squashy.) Cover the ground and chopped vegetables with the salt and let stand for three hours. Drain well. Mix the celery and mustard seeds through the pickle. Scald the vinegar with the sugar, making sure the sugar is all dissolved. Put the pickle into your crock or jars, pour the scalding hot vinegar over it and the pickle is made. Cover tight and set by till ready to use it. Cooking isn't necessary.—*J. Butterfield, Proprietor, The Country Club Inn, Harford County.*

AMBER MARMALADE

Slice thin one grape fruit, one orange, one lemon, using everything but seeds and cores. Measure fruit and put in three times the quantity of water. Let stand overnight. Next morning boil for ten minutes only. Let stand until next morning, when add pint for pint of sugar. Let boil steadily, stirring as little as possible, until it jellies, which should be about two hours. One good way to test is to hold spoon so that liquid drops from the side of the bowl, and when two or three drops hold without falling it is done. To secure best results select best fruit only, none too ripe.—*Miss Louisa Ogle Thomas, Baltimore.*

HIGDON PICKLE

Cut as many cucumbers in pieces the size of dice as will fill a large tureen, with one-third as many onions cut in the same way. Mix in a handful of salt and let it stand five or six hours; then strain them through a sieve until they are quite dry. As you put them in the jar, sprinkle with cayenne pepper, about four teaspoonsful will be enough, a little mace beaten fine, one gill of sweet oil, one pint of Madeira wine. Fill the jar with vinegar and tie it up.—*Miss Amelia H. Birnie, Carroll County.*

MARTYNIA PICKLE

Put Martynias in brine strong enough to bear an egg. Stand one week. Drain and put in vinegar for another week. Drain.

Mix these ingredients: one gallon vinegar, three pounds brown sugar, one-half cup of allspice (whole), one cup whole cloves, one half cup whole black pepper-corns, two tablespoons celery seed, eight pods red pepper.

Boil all these in vinegar. Pour over Martynias while hot. Horse-radish may be added if desired. Keep six months before using.—*Mrs. Anne Merryman Carroll, Hayfields, Baltimore County.*

PRESERVED ORANGES

Take the oranges, carve them handsomely, taking care not to cut through to the juices; boil them in water until you can run a straw through the skin. Then weigh three pounds of sugar, 1 pound of oranges and take half this quantity of sugar and make a syrup; boil them until nearly clear and then add the rest of the sugar and boil them until you think they are done. Then take the oranges out and boil the syrup hard an hour longer, seasoning them with mace and white vinegar.—*Mrs. Wm. H. Thomas, Carroll County.*

CUCUMBER PICKLE

One-half a gallon of vinegar, three pounds of sugar, two tablespoonsful of cloves, two tablespoonsful of allspice, two tablespoonsful of mustard, two tablespoonsful of celery seed, one tablespoonful of white ginger, one tablespoonful of cinnamon, one tablespoonful of black pepper, two pods of green pepper, a little garlic, horseradish, and four lemons sliced thin. Take twelve onions and as many cucumbers as the prepared vinegar will cover (about sixty-five), and boil together until done.—*Mr. and Mrs. J. Spence Howard, Sotterley, St. Mary's County.*

"Straw-Bay-Rees! Straw-Bay-Rees! Ann-Ran'l Straw-Bay-Rees!"

STRAWBERRY JAM

(J. FRED ESSARY *is recognized as one of the most astute political writers of the day. It has been his lot "to travel in America and Europe over 300,000 miles with Presidents from Roosevelt to Coolidge." Aside from his political writings as Washington Correspondent of the Baltimore "Sun," he has written, among other books, "Covering Washington," "Reverse English," "Maryland in National Politics" and in collaboration with his wife has just completed a "Washington Sketch Book.")*

This receipt for strawberry jam will make a remarkably clear, red product. The berries remain almost whole and their juice thickens to a thin jelly.

Never cook more than two quarts at a time; one is better.

Select dry red fruit. Discard all soft or green berries. Remove caps, wash and drain slightly.

For one box of berries, add two cups of sugar, *no water.*

Cook slowly over moderate heat, about ten minutes, perhaps a little longer if the berries are very watery. Do not stir or mash with spoon, but watch carefully.

When jam is finished, the juice will have the thickness of thin jelly. Test by setting spoonful on ice and if the surface of the juice wrinkles, the jelly is done.—*J. F. Essary, Baltimore.*

PIGS' FOOT SOUSE

Take 6 pigs' feet, boil until meat leaves the bone. Take out of liquor, remove bone, and replace meat and skin in liquor.

Heat ¾ cup of good vinegar, add a tablespoonful of whole cloves, ¼ teaspoonful salt, dash of pepper, one bay-leaf. Pour over pigs' feet, set in a bowl to chill and jell; when cold skim off surplus fat, slice and serve cold.—*Mrs. Oliver Lyman Tunis, Baltimore.*

INDIA CHUTNEY SAUCE

Cut two quarts of green tomatoes in thin slices, take out seeds, sprinkle with three tablespoons of salt and let stand overnight. In morning drain through colander, put in porcelain kettle, add two quarts of sour apples peeled and chopped fine, two chopped green peppers, one pound seeded raisins, two pints good cider vinegar. Simmer for two hours, then add one pound brown sugar, one pint lemon juice, three tablespoons of mustard seed, two tablespoons of ginger, one teaspoon paprika and cook slowly for another hour. Put in glass fruit jars and when cold wrap in paper and keep in cool place.—*The Misses Reynolds, Rose Hill Manor Inn, Frederick County.*

SPANISH PICKLES

One peck green tomatoes; one dozen onions. Slice and sprinkle with salt, let stand all night, then strain off juice. Allow one pound brown sugar; one-quarter pound white mustard seed; one ounce ground black pepper; one ounce cloves; one ounce ginger; one ounce cinnamon (all ground). Put layers of tomatoes and onions and sprinkle with spice. Cover with vinegar and boil slowly for two hours. Pack in small jars.—*Mrs. J. Morsell Roberts, Calvert County.*

QUINCE PASTE

Boil the fruit whole till tender, then pare and core and press through a sieve. To every pound of fruit put one of sugar, boil fifteen or twenty minutes and spread on dishes for six days. Sprinkle sugar over it and turn it every other day, then put in jars.—*Mrs. Wm. H. Thomas, Carroll County.*

TOMATO CATSUP

One gallon of tomato juice, pulp and seeds strained off, four tablespoonsful of salt, four tablespoonsful of allspice, four tablespoonsful of cloves, one tablespoonful of mustard, four tablespoonsful of black pepper, eight pods of red pepper, one teaspoonful of cayenne pepper. These spices to be bruised fine and simmered in one quart of vinegar and added to the tomatoes after they have been boiled to one-half.

The pepper pods to be boiled *with* the tomatoes.—*Dr. Walter Forman Wickes, Wickcliffe, Greenspring Valley, Baltimore County.*

CONSERVED WATERMELON RIND

Use only the white of the rind, taking care to remove all the red and green. Cut rind in small squares or any fancy shapes you prefer. Cover pieces with cold water and add teaspoonful powdered alum to make it firm. Let stand overnight. In the morning pour all the water off and cover with fresh water to which add one heaping tablespoonful ginger. Boil one-half hour, remove pieces of rind and rinse in fresh water. Make syrup of three quarts water, five pounds of sugar and the juice of five lemons. Cut lemon skins in small pieces and add to syrup. Also add to syrup two tablespoonsful whole mace. Boil syrup about five minutes, then add six or seven pounds of melon rind and boil until clear and syrup thickens. Skim often. Fill jars full to the brim with fruit and syrup and make air tight.—*Mrs. Ida Kenney, Baltimore.*

255

PUDDINGS

BERRY PUDDING

ONE quart of blackberries or huckleberries, or such berries as may be desired, one quart of bread crumbs, one quart of milk, three eggs, one-half cup of butter, one cup of sugar. Soak the crumbs in the milk for an hour. Cream the butter, add sugar, then put in the eggs, and then fruit. Bake a half an hour. Serve with hard sauce made of one cup of powdered sugar, one-quarter cup of butter. Cream together and add one well-beaten white of egg. Season with sherry wine or vanilla.—*Mrs. James B. Parran, Deep Falls, St. Mary's County.*

CARAMEL PUDDING

One cup butter, one cup sugar, five eggs (yolks and whites beaten separately), one cup preserved damsons strained and mashed, one teaspoon vanilla.

Cream butter and sugar, add eggs and damsons. Beat well together and bake on pastry.—*Mrs. George H. Birnie, Carroll County.*

BLACKBERRY PUDDING

4 eggs, 3½ cups flour, 2½ cups sugar, ½ cup butter, ½ cup milk, 1 quart berries, ½ glass wine, ½ nutmeg, ½ teaspoon soda.

Mix butter and sugar, add yolks of eggs, then milk, in which the soda has been dissolved, then a part of flour and whites of eggs, well beaten. Sift other half of flour over berries, then add nutmeg and wine. Bake. Serve with hard sauce. Huckleberries may be substituted for blackberries.—*Miss Margaretta Hollyday, Ratcliffe Manor, Talbot County.*

RATCLIFFE MANOR

(WHAT *a quiet dignity pervades "Ratcliffe Manor"! What memories it suggests!
Built about 1747 by Col. James Hollyday, it has seen life enjoyed in all its
finer aspects. Here in the old days hospitality ruled supreme.*

*Among Maryland families "duties" and "chores" meant to the slaves just
another opportunity to help the "massa" or "missus" or maybe the "missy."
Pleasing guests was an endeavor confined not only to the manorial hosts but
enjoyed by the faithful black retinue as well.*

*In the old Manors such as "Ratcliffe," life was gay, carefree and pulsating
with the keen joy of living, living better than it has since been possible on this
side of the Atlantic. "Ratcliffe Manor" represents American Georgian architecture
and American Georgian life at their best.*)

INDIAN PUDDING

Scald two quarts of skim milk. Stir in Indian meal enough
to make thin mush. Add a little salt, a tablespoonful of ginger
or any spice, a teacup of molasses, a lump of butter. Bake in a
tin or earthen pan two hours.—*The Misses Lelia and Alice Taney,
Frederick County.*

APPLE PUDDING

Mash well three pints of stewed apples, melt one pound of butter and beat ten eggs with two pounds of sugar. Mix all together with a glass of brandy. Add nutmeg to taste. Bake in pie crust.—*Mrs. Emerson C. Harrington, Jr., Dorchester County.*

BATTER PUDDING

Beat five eggs separately. To each egg add a heaping tablespoon of flour. Mix flour and yolks with enough milk to make a stiff batter. Beat until very light, then add one and one half pints of milk, and then the whites, well beaten, one tablespoon of yeast powder, and butter the size of a large egg. Bake in a quick oven in an old-time yellow pan.—*Mrs. James B. Parran, Deep Falls, St. Mary's County.*

CALIFORNIA PUDDING

One large can of pineapple (chopped not too fine), one quarter pound butter, one and one-half cups brown sugar, stew in iron frying pan until syrup is thick, then add one cup pecan nut meat. Cool.

Cake part: Three eggs, one cup white sugar, one cup flour, one teaspoonful yeast powder, three tablespoonsful boiling water. Pour on first mixture, cook in moderate oven twenty minutes. Turn out into plate and serve with whipped cream.—*Miss Mary McDaniel, Talbot County.*

READBOURNE

(The *original grant of the plantation known as "Readbourne" dates back as far as 1659, when it was granted to George Read. Later it came into the possession of the Hollyday family who held it through seven generations, a period of one hundred and sixty-eight years. Col. James Hollyday was the first of his family to own it and started the present manor house in 1731. The house was frequently referred to as "Readbourne Iron Chest" because Col. Hollyday was known to keep the funds of the Eastern Shore, of which he was treasurer during the seventeen forties, in an old English made ironbound chest within the walls of this sturdy stronghold. While it is quite frequently claimed that much brick used during the colony and pre-revolution days was brought over from England, facts and history shed much doubt of such procedure as a practice as Maryland clay proved so reliably fitting for brick making. It seems however that Readbourne was one of the exceptions to the rule and much brick for building was brought over from England along with other shipments for the comforts and luxury of the proprietors of Readbourne.)*

COCONUT BREAD PUDDING

1 pint milk, 2 cups diced bread (stale), light measure, ½ cup grated coconut, 2 eggs, 1 tablespoon butter, ½ cup sugar or sweeten to taste, ¼ teaspoon salt, 1 teaspoon vanilla.

Scald the milk and soak the bread in it for an hour or more. Stir butter in while hot, also sugar. When cool add yolks of egg, and coconut. Beat whites thoroughly and add. Put in greased baking dish and place in pan of water. Bake about thirty minutes. Serve hot or cold with cream.—*Readbourne Receipts, Queen Anne's County (Courtesy of Misses Clara and Bessie Hollyday)*.

CHOCOLATE CREAM PUDDING

Put two ounces of chocolate into a double boiler. When melted add a pint of hot milk, two and a half cupfuls of sugar; stir until thoroughly mixed, then add a teaspoonful of vanilla. Moisten two tablespoonsful of corn starch; cook until smooth and thick. Now stir in the well-beaten yolks of four eggs. Turn this into the serving dish. Beat the whites of the eggs until they are light, but not stiff; add four tablespoonsful of powdered sugar and beat until stiff and light; heap them over the pudding, dust thickly with powdered sugar and stand the dish on a board, and then in the oven until the upper portion of the pudding is crusted a golden brown.—*Miss Eliza Thomas, Baltimore*.

HAMPTON FROZEN PUDDING

3 quarts of cream, 2 cups of sugar, 3 tablespoons of rum, 9 tablespoons of sherry, 1 quart jar of preserved cherries, 3 dozen macaroons.

Stir sugar in gradually. Stir in sherry and rum so it won't curdle, then cherries (drained juice), and last 3 dozen stale macaroons broken into 3 or 4 pieces. Freeze and serve.—*John Ridgely, Hampton, Baltimore County*.

CORN MEAL PUDDING

2 kitchen cups of corn meal, 6 eggs, yolks and whites beaten separately, 2 quarts boiled milk stirred gradually while hot into the corn meal, 1 quart of molasses, 2 lemons, rinds grated and the juice, 1 nutmeg, 1 teaspoonful of allspice, cloves, cinnamon, ⅛ pound of butter, 2 tablespoons of brown sugar.

Boil milk, stir into the corn meal and mix well, then stir in butter while the milk is hot, then the brown sugar, spices, molasses, lemon and lastly the yolks and whites of the eggs.

½ teaspoon of Sterling Yeast Powder (baking powder). Bake an hour and a half in a moderate oven. Serve with whipped cream, or creamed butter and sugar sauce.—*John Ridgely, Hampton, Baltimore County.*

FIG PUDDING

Six ounces of suet, six ounces of bread crumbs, six ounces of sugar, one-half pound of figs, 3 eggs, one cup of milk, one half cup of brandy, two tablespoonsful baking powder. Steam three hours.—*Miss Eliza Thomas, Baltimore.*

PLUM PUDDING BASE

(*To insure a light pudding*)

Two cups stale cake crumbs, two eggs, one cup milk, pinch of salt, teaspoon of yeast powder. Steam three hours in a double boiler. Then add any combination of fruits or spices and the result will always be light and a guarantee against indigestion.—*Miss Mary McDaniel, Talbot County.*

DELMONICO PUDDING

Three tablespoons corn starch, one quart of milk, yolks of five eggs beaten with six tablespoons of sugar, flavored with vanilla. Mix the starch with cold milk, stir it into the quart of milk just before it boils, then add the eggs and sugar, set it in the oven to stiffen enough to hold the frosting. Beat the whites to a froth, with three tablespoons of sugar, and flavor with vanilla, pour the frosting on the pudding, set it in the oven to brown a little; to be eaten cold.—*Mrs. Wm. Courtland Hart, Somerset County.*

DIXIE PUDDING

Soak one pint of fresh bread crumbs in one quart of warm milk with piece of butter the size of an egg.

Beat the yolks of four eggs with one cup of sugar until very light and add to milk and bread with the grated rind of one lemon.

Bake in pudding dish for twenty minutes. Take from fire and spread currant jelly. Cover with meringue and return for one minute to hot oven.

Meringue

Whites of four eggs, one tablespoon of water, beat until dry, add four tablespoons sugar and a few drops of vanilla. Drop by tablespoon on the currant jelly. Serve cold with cream seasoned with sherry wine.—*John H. Sothoron, The Plains, St. Mary's County.*

ENGLISH PLUM PUDDING

One cup bread crumbs, one cup flour, one-half cup butter, one cup brown sugar, one teaspoon salt, two teaspoonsful baking powder, one teaspoonful mixed spices, three eggs, one cup milk, one cup seeded raisins, one-half cup chopped citron, one half cup preserved ginger, one cup currants, one-half cup brandy, one-half cup chopped nuts.

Mix flour with bread crumbs, add butter, sugar, salt and baking powder, spices, nuts, milk, fruit, eggs beaten light and brandy. Steam four hours.—*Mrs. Eloise Hance, Calvert County.*

ELLIN NORTH PLUM PUDDING

(THIS *receipt was handed down from Mrs. John Moale (Ellin North) to her great-grandson the late Walter de Curzon Poultney. Ellin North, born in 1740, is generally reputed to have been the first white child born in Baltimore. Her father, a wealthy landed proprietor, at one time owned the ground at present occupied by the modern Hotel Emerson. Ellin North was a woman of striking personality and her husband, Col. John Moale, one of the town's most worthy citizens, was Colonel of the Baltimore Town Militia.*)

One lb. raisins, one lb. currants, one half lb. citron, one lb. suet (white), one tablespoon salt, one and one-half nutmegs, one lb. sugar, one wineglass brandy, eight eggs, one pint milk, one pint bread crumbs, four or five apples, one tablespoon flour, one heaping tablespoon of ginger. Pick seeded raisins apart. Wash currants and dry them thoroughly. Chop citron into small pieces. Chop and shred suet. Cut apples into small pieces. Crumb inside of stale loaf of bread, and measure loosely a light pint. Mix salt and spices with bread crumbs. Make batter of eggs, milk, sugar, flour and bread crumbs. Have the fruit floured, and add apples and suet to batter. Put the brandy in last. Take a square yard of heavy unbleached muslin (well washed and dried), lay it on large dish or tray, grease heavily with lard a round space of about one-half yard in diameter, then sift thickly with flour. Pour pudding in, holding up corners, and gather quickly together the edges. Tie with strong string, having enough space for pudding to swell. Put plate in bottom of large pot to prevent pudding from touching bottom. Boil for three hours.

Sauce

To 12 tablespoons of granluated sugar and one quarter pound of butter creamed together add two well-beaten eggs. Heat and mix until smooth, no longer. Add cup of sherry and serve.—*Dr. J. Hall Pleasants, author of "Maryland Silversmiths 1715-1830," Baltimore.*

ENGLISH PLUM PUDDING

Two pounds of raisins, two pounds of currants, one-half pound citron, two pounds of suet, one-half pound of flour, one-half pound of bread crumbs, one pound of brown sugar, four glasses of brandy, sixteen eggs. Boil one hour.—*Mr. and Mrs. J. Spence Howard, St. Mary's Manor, St. Mary's County.*

PUDDING OF SPLIT RUSKS

Pour some boiling milk over sixteen split rusks, then add a quarter pound of butter, a quarter pound of almonds, six eggs, sugar and lemon peel, and lastly add the whites of the eggs beaten to a froth. Bake and serve it up with a wine sauce.—*Mrs. Wm. D. Poultney, Baltimore.*

FREDERIC ARNOLD KUMMER

(IN *meeting that genial son of Maryland in his hospitable Baltimore home,
with its atmosphere of past generations and its spirit of modernity, one might
not suspect that, like another celebrated Baltimorean, the late F. Hopkinson
Smith, Mr. Kummer, too, turned from notable success in the field of engineer-
ing (he is a Corporate Member of The American Society of Civil Engineers)
to the brush for self-expression, saw his pictures hung in two annual exhibi-
tions of The Pennsylvania Academy of the Fine Arts, and then proceeded to
win international fame as a writer through his many plays, books and short
stories. In addition to American publication his works have appeared in England, Germany, Norway, Sweden, Spain and other foreign countries; his plays
include musical comedies with both Sigmund Romberg and the late Victor
Herbert; his books, from that brilliant novel "Ladies in Hades" to his three-
volume work for children, "The Earth's Story," have attained widespread popu-
larity in their individual fields, he has been a frequent contributor to all the
better magazines, and much of his work has appeared on the screen.*)

PLUM PUDDING

Small salt spoonful of salt, one-half nutmeg grated, juice and grated rind of one lemon, one pound of raisins seeded, one pound of currants, one pint of bread crumbs, one pint of milk, four eggs, one cup of chopped suet, one cup of flour.

Wash fruit and dry, then mix it with the flour. Beat the eggs, add suet, bread crumbs, lemon, nutmeg, salt and milk, stirring in the fruit last. Place mixture in a floured muslin bag, through which the water cannot penetrate, or in a floured pewter mold. Cover with water and boil for four hours. Allow two inches for swelling. Serve with clear brandy, lighted, or with brandy sauce (hard).

For the hard sauce, take one half cup of butter, two cups powdered sugar, two sherry glasses of brandy, one teaspoonful of mixed cinnamon and mace. Warm the butter very slightly, work in the sugar, and when this is light, the brandy and the spices. Beat hard, shape in mold, and set in cool place until needed.

This plum pudding receipt was given me by my great-grandmother, who was born in Baltimore in 1800, and died in 1888, when I was a small boy. She remembered the bombardment of Fort McHenry very well, and stood on Federal Hill with her mother and some other children watching it, and whenever one of the bombs missed, or fell short, they all clapped their hands. This was while Francis Scott Key was writing "The Star-Spangled Banner" as a prisoner on one of the British ships. She also said that in the morning they saw Wells and McComas go out to shoot General Ross.—*Frederic Arnold Kummer, Baltimore.*

PLUM PUDDING

(As made in the home of Governor Thomas Nelson of Yorktown, Virginia)

One pound of beef suet chopped very fine, one and a half pounds of raisins, one and a half pounds of currants, one-half pound of bread crumbs, one-half pound of brown sugar, six eggs, one wine glass of wine, one wine glass of brandy, one teaspoonful of nutmeg, one teaspoonful of ground mace. Beats eggs and sugar together, then add flour, spice, wine, brandy, bread crumbs and last of all the fruit well flavored. Put in a pudding mold and boil four hours. Water must be boiling when pudding is put in.—*Mr. Alexander C. Nelson, Baltimore.*

PLUM PUDDING

10 puddings of moderate size. Beat up 5 dozen eggs, add to them: 6 lbs. seeded raisins, a little chopped, 4 lbs. currants, 1 lb. sliced citron, 6 lbs. suet, chopped not very fine, 4 lbs. sugar, 4 loaves bread, grated, 1 tablespoon mace, ½ pint brandy. Ground ginger to taste and a little salt.

Dust the fruit well with flour, before mixing and then mix all the above well together. Dip the cloths in which you intend to put the puddings, in hot water. Wring them out and dust them well with flour. Tie the bags very tight, so as to exclude the water, but leave room for them to swell. Boil them 4 hours. Take them out of the water and hang them up in a dry airy place, not allowing them to touch each other. When wanted, boil them ½ hour. To be eaten with the usual sauce. When prepared for the table they are improved by sticking citron, cut in thin slices, over the top.—*Mrs. E. Glenn Perine, Baltimore.*

REBEL PUDDING

Three cups of flour, two of milk, one of molasses, one of butter, two of fruit, spice at pleasure. Boil in a bag for two hours.
—*Mrs. Wm. H. Thomas, Carroll County.*

QUEEN OF PUDDINGS

1 quart of milk, 1 quart diced bread (stale) light measure, 1 cup sugar, 4 egg yolks, rind of 1 lemon grated, butter the size of an egg.

Scald the milk and soak the bread in it for an hour or more. Stir butter in while hot, also sugar. When cooked add yolks of eggs and lemon rind. Put in greased baking dish and bake about thirty minutes.

When done spread top with preserves, any kind desired, raspberry was usually used at "Readbourne," then add meringue of egg whites and place in oven until brown. Serve cold with cream.—*Readbourne Receipts, Queen Anne's County. (Courtesy of Misses Clara and Bessie Hollyday.)*

SUET PUDDING

Three cupfuls of flour, one cupful of chopped suet, one teaspoonful of salt. Stir one teaspoonful of soda into one cupful of molasses and add one cupful of milk. Combine the two mixtures then add two cupfuls of floured fruit, raisins, citron and currants mixed. Half fill a covered pudding mold and steam for three hours. Serve with sauce.—*Miss Julia Loker, Mulberry Fields, St. Mary's County.*

SWEET POTATO PUDDING OR PIE

1 pint boiled and mashed sweet potatoes. To this add butter the size of an egg, 1½ cups of sugar, the grated rind of a lemon and juice of same, the yolks of three eggs and beat well. Then add 1½ cups of milk and lastly the well beaten whites of the eggs. This can be baked either in pastry shells or a greased dish as a pudding.—*Readbourne Receipts, Queen Anne's County. (Courtesy of Swepson Earle.)*

TAPIOCA PUDDING

Five dessertspoons of tapioca, one quart of milk, one pint of cold water, three eggs, one cup of sugar, a pinch of salt, one teaspoon of vanilla. Soak the tapioca in cold water overnight. Bake in pudding dish.—*Mrs. William T. Delaplaine, Frederick County.*

DESSERTS

DR. JOHNSON (*upon regarding a French menu*):—"*Sir, my brain is obfuscated after the perusal of this heterogeneous conglomeration of bastard English ill-spelt, and a foreign tongue.*
"*I prithee bid thy knaves bring me a dish of hog's puddings, a slice or two from the upper cut of a well-roasted sirloin, and two apple-dumplings.*"

APPLE DUMPLING

One and a half pints of flour, one teacup lard, mix well and moisten with warm water. Take one teacupful of butter and put over the rolled flour in little bits till used up. Pare and cut apples in small pieces—roll pastry the size wished. Put in apples and tie up in a cloth leaving room to swell. Put in boiling water, keeping pot full. Cook four hours.—*Miss Louisa Ogle Thomas, St. Mary's County.*

BLACKBERRY FLUMMERY

Stew three pints of blackberries with a pint of sugar for fifteen minutes. Thicken with cornstarch and pour into individual molds. Serve with whipped cream on top when cold.—*Mrs. Emerson C. Harrington, Jr. Dorchester County.*

BAKED APPLES

Get red apples, peel and bake, filling the holes where core came from with raisins. Take the peelings and a few apples, put on the fire with a very little water. Drain off the juice as done to make jelly, add to a cup of juice a cup of sugar, boil until it will jell when a little is put on a cold plate. Put the apples in the dish they are to be served in, and pour the juice over and around the apples, let stand in a cold place until it jellies and serve with cream.—*As prepared twenty-five years ago by Grace's Quarter Ducking Club, Gun Powder River, Baltimore County; Mr. Alexander C. Nelson, Baltimore.*

BLACKBERRY CUSTARD

1 lb. sugar, ¼ lb. butter, 6 eggs (beaten separately). Flavor with oil of lemon and vanilla. Cream butter very light, add sugar and eggs separately. Put pastry in pans and brown a little. Put blackberry preserve in pans, then pour on custard. Bake a light brown.—*Mrs. Irving Adams, Howard County.*

CHARLOTTE RUSSE

½ box of gelatine dissolved in about ½ cup of water. When dissolved beat up the yolks of 6 eggs and a good sized cup of sugar. Put in with gelatine in a double saucepan and cook until eggs are cooked. Pour out in large bowl to cool, while it cools beat up one quart of cream and keep stirring in until cold enough to mold. Flavor with vanilla. Set lady-fingers in the tin or china mold, then pour on mixture and set away in a cool place. —*John Ridgely, Hampton, Baltimore County.*

CAFE PARFAIT

One quart thick cream, one gill black coffee, one-half cup of powdered sugar. Add the coffee and sugar to the cream, then whip the whole to a froth, as fast as the froth comes to the surface, skim it off and place in a colander to drain. That which drains off may be turned back and whipped over. When it is all whipped, turn it carefully into an ice-cream mold, press the lid down tightly, bind the joint with a strip of buttered muslin, pack in ice and salt and let stand three hours to freeze. Chocolate parfait may be made in the same way, also it may be made of fruit.—*Mrs. J. Alexis Shriver, Olney, Harford County.*

BROWN BETTY

1 cup of bread crumbs or slices of bread, 2 cups of chopped tart apples, ½ cup of brown sugar, 1 teaspoon of cinnamon (or ½ teaspoon of nutmeg), 1 lemon grated instead if desired, 2 tablespoons of butter.

Butter a deep dish. Put in a layer of apples at the bottom. Sprinkle with sugar, a few bits of butter and the flavoring, a layer of bread crumbs and so on until the dish is filled. The bread crumbs should be a little thicker at the top. Cover it closely and steam three quarters of an hour in a moderate oven, then uncover and let it brown quickly. Eat with butter and sugar, sauce or cream.—*John Ridgely, Hampton, Baltimore County.*

CHOCOLATE BLANC MANGE

1 quart of milk, 1 pinch of soda, 1 cup of sugar, 4 tablespoonfuls cornstarch, 4 tablespoonfuls grated chocolate, 1 teaspoonful of vanilla.

Heat the milk and add the soda. Into the milk stir the sugar. When dissolved add the cornstarch wet with cold milk. Cook until smooth and very thick. Add grated chocolate and cook for a minute before removing from fire. Stir in the vanilla, turn into a mold moistened with cold water and set in a cold place to form.—*Dining Car Service, B. & O. R.R.*

SPANISH CREAM

Soak one envelope of Knox's Gelatine in one quart of milk ten minutes—put on fire. Stir until dissolved. Add yolks of three eggs and four tablespoons sugar well beaten. Cook in double boiler. Have egg whites well beaten with four tablespoons of sugar. Add whites stirring until mixed. Flavor with one teaspoonful vanilla. Add one teaspoon salt. Turn into wet molds.—*Miss Eloise Hance, Calvert County.*

COFFEE BAVARIAN CREAM

One-half box of gelatine, one-half pint of milk, one pint cream, one teaspoon of vanilla, one cup of sugar, one cup of strong boiling coffee. Cover the gelatine with cold water and let it soak for half an hour, then pour over it the boiling coffee. Add the sugar and stir until it is dissolved. Then strain into a basin. Let stand until cool. While it is cooling whip the cream. When cool add first the milk and then the whipped cream. Stir carefully until thoroughly mixed. Turn into a mold and set away to harden.—*Miss Eliza Thomas, Baltimore.*

LEMON CREAM

Take eight eggs and a half a pint of wine, the juice of two lemons, sweeten to your taste, stir all together leaving out the whites of eggs, which when beaten to a froth, may be stirred in when the other ingredients have commenced boiling. Do not let it remain but a few minutes on the fire after it boils.—*Mrs. Wm. D. Poultney, Baltimore.*

DATE DELIGHT

2 cups dates, 1 cup chopped walnuts, ¼ cup crystallized ginger, 1½ tablespoonsful lemon juice, ¼ cup cherries, whipped cream. Pit dates and cut in pieces, break nuts into pieces, cut ginger and halve the cherries. Combine all with lemon juice. Chill. When ready to serve arrange in sherbet glasses and top with whipped cream. Garnish with whole cherries.—*Mrs. J. H. Windsor, Windsor Manor, Baltimore County.*

DOLLY IN THE BLANKETS

Two cups of flour, three teaspoons of baking powder, half a cup of lard. Mix with water making dough as soft as you can handle and roll out like pie crust. Cover all over with berries or soft peaches sliced. Sprinkle over with sugar and dot with butter. Roll up, put in a cloth which has been scalded and then put in boiling water. Cook slowly for half an hour. Don't leave it in the water when done. Use any kind of sauce, whiskey sauce preferred.—*Mrs. Charles Wickes Whaland, Kent County.*

FLOATING ISLAND

Have the bowl nearly full of syllabub made with milk, white wine and sugar; beat the whites of six eggs to a strong froth then mix with it raspberry or strawberry marmalade, enough to flavor and color it. Lay the froth on the syllabub, first putting in some slices of cake. Raise it in little mounds and garnish it with something light.—*Mrs. Wm. H. Thomas, Carroll County.*

CHOCOLATE MOUSSE

Whip one quart of cream to a very stiff froth. Sprinkle over two-thirds of a cupful of powdered sugar; mix carefully and then add two ounces of melted chocolate, or if you like you may use sweet chocolate, sprinkled into the cream. Mix carefully, add a teaspoonful of vanilla, put the mixture into a melon mold, put on the lid and bind the space with a strip of muslin. Pack in salt ice and allow to freeze from two and a half to three hours.—*Miss Eliza Thomas, Baltimore.*

STRAWBERRY SURPRISE

Crush one quart of fruit to pulp, cover with one pint granulated sugar. Pour on this a half pint of cold water, and the unbeaten whites of five eggs. Mix and turn in freezer. The grinding process will whip the contents in frozen foam, light yet firm.—*Mrs. Charles B. Trail, Frederick County.*

PEPPERMINT ICE CREAM

One quart of double cream, one dozen sticks of red and white candy peppermint. Let stand all night. In morning, mash in cream and strain. Sweeten to taste, add two drops of oil of peppermint, freeze. Serve with chocolate sauce. (This receipt is of German origin.)—*Miss Margaret Lentz Miller, Garrett County.*

CARAMEL ICE CREAM

2 quarts milk, 7 eggs, 1 tablespoon flour. Boil 1½ lbs. brown sugar, 1 tablespoon water, boil until it bubbles, when cool add to the custard above. Whip 3 pints cream and add to above mixture with 1 teaspoon vanilla and freeze.—*Mrs. Marion T. Hargis, Worcester County.*

FROZEN STRAWBERRIES

One quart berries, one cup water. Boil ten minutes and strain through colander, add one cup sugar. Freeze partly, add juice of one lemon, whites of three eggs beaten stiff and one pint cream and freeze solid.—*Mrs. E. W. Humphreys, Wicomico County.*

ST. MARY'S MANOR

(BUILT *in 1820 by Dr. J. Thomas Brome, grandfather of Mrs. J. Spence Howard, on the site of the original grant to Leonard Calvert in 1634 known as Governor's Field. It was the first patent in Maryland. Here the first grist mill was built on this side of the Atlantic, the old mill stones of which now repose on the grounds of St. Mary's Manor.*)

PEACH FOAM

Put a cupful of fine peaches, cut into small bits after peeling, into a bowl with half a cup of powdered sugar. Beat for a while with a silver fork, then add the white of one egg well beaten. Beat all together for half an hour. Chill in the refrigerator and serve with cream, either whipped or plain. This is a delicate and tempting dish for an invalid.—*Mr. and Mrs. J. Spence Howard, St. Mary's Manor, St. Mary's County.*

ICE CREAM (VANILLA)

Boil one quart of new milk or cream with vanilla or lemon peel. Then pour it on 2 egg yolks well beaten, stirring all the time. Sweeten it to taste, return it to the skillet, boil about 10 minutes, stirring all the time. When it is cold, freeze it as usual.— *Receipt of the sisters Sophonisba and Angelica Peale, daughters of Charles Willson Peale, preëminent artist of the era of the American Revolution.*

PEACH MOUSSE

½ envelope of Knox's gelatine, ¼ cup of cold water, 1 cup of cream, 1 cup of sugar, ¼ cup of lemon juice, 1 quart of peaches. Soak gelatine in cold water, a few minutes before dissolving in hot water. Cut up peaches, cover with sugar and lemon juice, let stand one hour. Mash and rub through a strainer. Add dissolved gelatine. Add whipped cream and beat until stiff. Pour in mold and pack in ice and salt. Let stand four hours. This applies to all fruit just the same.—*Mrs. W. B. Deen, Caroline County.*

PRUNE SOUFFLÉ

Twenty-eight prunes. Boil until a soft mass then put through the colander with a little juice. Whites of six eggs beaten to a very stiff froth, four teaspoonsful of sugar. Then whip prunes and whites of eggs beaten until very stiff. Put in a baking dish and set dish in a pan of boiling water and bake for fifteen minutes. Then serve either hot or cold with whipped cream.—*Mrs. Bartlett S. Johnston, Baltimore.*

TOM THUMB

(The *Baltimore & Ohio, the only railroad in the country having enjoyed a century of existence, has always taken pride in upholding and spreading the gastronomic reputation of the city whose name it bears. The menu of one of the most elaborate repasts given in Baltimore is included in the appendix. It was used upon the occasion of the Great Railway Celebration of 1857—a year made famous by one of the worst economic and financial panics this country has ever experienced—and chronicled a sumptuous banquet given the first train load of the citizens of St. Louis who traveled to Baltimore over its lines.*

From the time of its first diner the B & O has realized the value of Maryland's reputation for gastronomic superiority, and today in their diners, the first air-conditioned cars in use on any railroad, travelers from all parts of the country are enabled to enjoy their first taste of authentic Maryland cooking, by Southern colored cooks. Particular attention is given the dishes which have originated in the Great Chesapeake Bay.)

STRAWBERRY SHORTCAKE

1 quart sifted flour, 1 teaspoonful salt, 4 teaspoonsful baking powder, ½ cup Crisco, 2 cups milk. (Use more if necessary.)

Sift flour, salt and baking powder together. Then add the Crisco and last add the milk gradually—the dough should be soft as can be handled and without sticking; then turn it out on a floured molding board and knead lightly. Then roll to one inch thick and cut with a 3½ inch round cutter and lay them in a baking pan not touching each other and bake in a hot oven from 15 to 20 minutes. Just before serving split the cake and spread the bottom half with washed crushed sweetened strawberries and cover and spread the top half with the same.—*Dining Car Service, B. & O. R.R.*

WALKER PIE

Line a dish about 4 inches deep with pastry. Pare yellow peaches and put them on to cook. Add enough sugar to make them fairly sweet. Cook until good and rich, adding lump of butter while cooking. Pour into dish lined with pastry and cover with upper crust and cook for about ½ hour. Serve warm with vanilla ice cream.—*Mrs. Irving Adams, Howard County.*

TIPSY SQUIRE

Take a loaf of sponge cake, stick the top full of blanched almonds and put into a large glass dish. Over this pour enough sherry or port wine to thoroughly saturate it, over all pour a rich custard.—*Miss Eliza Thomas, Baltimore.*

ORANGE SOUFFLE

1 quart cream, 1 lb. sugar, yolks of 6 eggs, ½ box gelatine, 1 pint orange juice. Soak gelatine 10 minutes in ½ cup cold water. Then add ½ cup hot water and stir until dissolved. Mix orange juice and sugar until they form a syrup. Beat yolks to a cream. Whip the cream. Now mix syrup and eggs together. Strain gelatine into it and stir carefully until it begins to thicken. Then stir in quickly the whipped cream and freeze. It should not be as hard as ice cream.—*Mrs. Charles B. Trail, Frederick County.*

BEVERAGES

A Marylander and a Virginian were discussing the merits of their respective liquors. The Marylander poured the Virginian two drinks. On imbibing one the Virginian fainted. When he came to, he admitted defeat. "But," said the Marylander, "you drank the chaser!"

BLACKBERRY CORDIAL

Pound and strain one gallon of berries, and to every pint of juice add three-quarters pound of sugar, and to every two quarts of juice one-quarter ounce each of mace, allspice, cinnamon, and cloves. Boil all to a rich syrup and fill bottles with equal parts of syrup and good spirits. Bottle and cork well.—*Miss Louisa Ogle Thomas, Baltimore.*

"Ah, perhaps to you, too, Nature has opened her sky picture page by page. Have you seen the lambent flame of dawn leaping across the livid east; the red-stained, sulphurous islets floating in the lake of fire in the west, the ragged clouds at midnight, black as a raven's wing, blotting out the shuddering moon?"

"Not since I give up drink."

CHERRY BOUNCE

Strain the juice of the cherries through a coarse cloth, then boil it, and put in cinnamon, lemon peel, cloves, allspice, mace and sugar (you are to be governed in the quantity of each by your taste). Then add one gallon of brandy to four of juice— at first it will be very strong, but in two months it will lose the strength and it will be necessary to add a quart of brandy to every four gallons of the bounce.—*Mrs. Wm. Courtland Hart, Somerset County.*

FRANKLIN FARMS EGGNOG

("FRANKLIN FARMS," *the old Howell House, or, as it was for many years known, the old "Howell-Carroll House," 3 West Franklin Street, Baltimore, was built for John Brown Howell of Baltimore, in the early part of the last century, about 1808. John Brown Howell was a son of William Howell of the important shipping firm of William Howell & Sons, whose ships were engaged in European and South American commerce, with headquarters at the Port of Baltimore and with offices in New Orleans and elsewhere.*

He had three daughters, one of whom married Charles Tucker Carroll, grandson of Charles Carroll of Carrollton, Jr., for whom his father Charles Carroll of Carrollton, the last surviving signer of the Declaration of Independence, built Homewood House, which is now owned by the Johns Hopkins University. The granddaughter of Charles Tucker Carroll married John Philip Hill, who for a number of years was a member of Congress from Maryland, residing at 3 West Franklin Street.

While Representative Hill was in Congress, he, in order to test the definition of "non-intoxicating" in Section 29 of the Volstead Act, turned the back yard of 3 West Franklin Street into "Franklin Farms" and caused a test case to be made in the United States Courts, which established a subsequent law for home-made cider and wine, that such home-made wine and cider could be made in the homes of citizens regardless of the actual alcoholic content.

For many years, there have been used in Howell House, or "Franklin Farms," two ancient receipts for Rum Punch and for Eggnog, which will be found in this volume.)

10 dozen eggs, 13 quarts cream (double) 9 quarts milk, 8¾ quarts spirits (1/3 brandy, 2/3 rum), 2½ pounds sugar.

Note: If ordinary cream, use all cream and no milk, that is, 22 quarts of cream. This will make 8½ gallons and just strong and thick enough. It is better to use all cream and no milk, but if double cream is used, the milk is all right.

The basic formula is:

1 egg, 1 wine glass cream, 1 wine glass spirits, 1 tablespoonful of sugar. (Spirits, 1/3 peach brandy, 2/3 jamaica rum, or all whiskey.)

The yolk of the eggs should be beaten hard and long, separately. The cream then slowly poured and stirred in. The sugar then stirred in and the spirits then added in a thin stream, the mass meanwhile being stirred. Half of the beaten whites are then stirred in and the other half of the whites beaten and poured on top. To make just two (2) gallons, use 2 dozen eggs, 4 quarts cream, 3 pints spirits, 1 pound sugar.—*John Philip Hill, Franklin Farms, Baltimore.*

BLACKBERRY BOUNCE

To every gallon juice put 2½ pounds sugar, one-half ounce cloves, one-half ounce cinnamon. Boil the whole to a thin jelly. When cold, to every quart of jelly add one-half pint whiskey or brandy; stir all well together and strain through a fine sieve and bottle for use.—*Mrs. J. Morsell Roberts, Calvert County.*

EGGNOG

One dozen eggs, separate and divide the whites into two parts. Beat yolks very light, add two tumblers of sugar, beat well, then add one quart of French cognac brandy and one pint of Jamaica rum, alternating very slowly at first. Now add three quarts of cream and one part of the beaten whites of eggs. Take the remaining whites, beat very stiff, add one cup of powdered sugar to make an icing, add to this one quart of cream and stir in above. This eggnog should be made the night before it is to be served, or long enough for the brandy and rum to blend.—*Mrs. Robert E. Tubman, Glasgow, Dorchester County.*

TOURIST: *"What precaution do you take against water pollution?"*
OLD RESIDENT: *"First we boils it."*
TOURIST: *"Good."*
OLD RESIDENT: *"Then we filters it."*
TOURIST: *"Splendid."*
OLD RESIDENT: *"Then we drinks beer."*

EGGNOG

12 eggs, separate whites from yolks, 12 tablespoons of sugar, 12 tablespoons French brandy, 12 tablespoons Jamaica rum. Beat yolks light and mix sugar thoroughly—add brandy and rum. Take one quart of cream and whip until stiff, add this to the other mixture. Beat whites stiff and add to the above ingredients. —*Colonel John Douglas Freeman, Charles and St. Mary's Counties.*

EGGNOG

Two quarts of cream, sixteen eggs, one pint of brandy, one pint of Jamaica spirits, one pound of loaf sugar. Beat the yolks light, and add the sugar and liquor slowly, then the cream. Beat the whites to a froth.—*Mr. and Mrs. J. Spence Howard, St. Mary's Manor, St. Mary's County.*

EGGNOG

1 doz. eggs, 1 gal. cream, 3 pts. brandy, 1 lb. sugar, ½ gal. milk, 1 pt. whiskey, 1/3 oz. ground nutmeg. Beat eggs and sugar together to a froth. Add all the other ingredients and pour from one vessel to another until thoroughly mixed and a deep froth stands on the mixture.—*Mr. Rudolph Kaiser, Anne Arundel County.*

MINT JULEP

Crush one lump of sugar at the bottom of a tall glass. Add half a dozen small sprigs of mint, which should first be lightly twisted between the fingers to break the skin of the leaves. Cover with whiskey and allow to stand for ten minutes. Then pour in balance of whiskey (to make a long drink a full whiskey glass should be used), fill the glass with finely crushed ice and stir rapidly with a spoon until the outside of the glass is frosted. Serve garnished with mint sprigs. The best Maryland juleps were made with old rye.—*Frederic Arnold Kummer, Baltimore.*

" 'Twould have been jolly well all right but for the damned weeds they put in them."

MINT CORDIAL

Fill a large kitchen bowl three-quarters full of *young* mint leaves (no stems)—cover with brandy. Let stay in broiling hot sun (July) all day. Strain, add sugar to taste. Bottle.—*John Ridgely, Hampton, Baltimore County.*

ARMY PUNCH

Two dozen lemons and two dozen oranges. One quart of light rum; three pounds of sugar; bottle and cork it and serve with crushed ice.—*Mrs. Wm. H. Thomas, Carroll County.*

WASHINGTON IRVING AND CHARLES DICKENS

(THAT *farewell dinner at Baltimore on March 23, 1842, was always a happy
memory with Dickens. During his second American tour he thus replied to a
letter from Mr. Charles Lanman:*

*"Your reference to my dear friend Washington Irving renews the vivid
impressions reawakened in my mind at Baltimore but the other day. I saw his
fine face for the last time in that city. He came there from New York to pass a
day or two with me before I went westward; and they were made among the
most memorable of my life by his delightful fancy and genial humour. Some
unknown admirer of his books and mine sent to the hotel a most enormous
mint julep, wreathed with flowers. We sat, one on either side of it, with great
solemnity (it filled a respectably-sized round table), but the solemnity was of
very short duration. It was quite an enchanted julep, and carried us among in-
numerable people and places that we both knew. The julep held out far into
the night, and my memory never saw him afterwards otherwise than as bend-
ing over it, with his straw, with an attempted air of gravity (after some anec-
dote involving some wonderfully droll and delicate observation of character),
and then as his eye caught mine, melting into that captivating laugh of his,
which was the brightest and best I have ever heard."—From "The Dickens
Circle," S. W. T. LEY.)*

PUNCH (VERY FINE)

Two tablespoons of red currant jelly in a teacup of water. One quart of brandy, one quart of whiskey, one quart of champagne, one and a half pints of strong green tea, the juice of six lemons, six lemons sliced, sugar to taste, ice additional.—*Mr. and Mrs. J. Spence Howard, St. Mary's Manor, St. Mary's County.*

FISH HOUSE PUNCH

One pint lemon juice, three pints mixture viz.:—One pint Jamaica spirits, one pint brandy and one pint peach brandy, four pounds sugar, nine pints of water. Make lemonade first, then add other liquors.—*Mrs. Charles H. Tilghman, Gross' Coate, Talbot County.*

FRANKLIN FARMS RUM PUNCH

12 lemons, 1¾ pounds lump sugar, 1 quart strong green unpowdered tea, 1 quart old Jamaica rum. Put sugar in large bowl and squeeze the juice of the lemons over the sugar; throw the rinds in another large bowl to use later—mixing the tea by scalding the teapot and putting in one-eighth pound of tea, fill the pot with boiling water and let this draw for twenty (20) minutes by the clock; pour one quart of hot tea over the lemon's rind and let stand for ten (10) minutes; then pour the hot tea from the rinds into the lemon juice and sugar. When the sugar is dissolved, pour in the quart of Jamaica rum and put in a demijohn and cork tightly. This should stand twenty-four (24) hours. Fill bowl with crushed ice and pour the punch over it.—*John Philip Hill, Franklin Farms, Baltimore.*

KENTUCKY BREAKFAST

*"Your water-drinking makes you useless to the state: whilst by my pota-
tions I increase the revenue."—"Bato in Athenæus,"* Epicurus.

TEA PUNCH

One pint rum, one and one-half cups sugar, six lemons, one
tablespoonful brandy, two cups strong tea. Peel the lemons thin
and pour the tea boiling hot over them. Squeeze the lemon juice
on the sugar and let remain an hour or more. Mix altogether and
pour over a bowl of crushed ice. This would serve about six
people before prohibition.—*Mrs. Anne Merryman Carroll, Hayfields, Baltimore County.*

Tourist Booking Agent: *"Naples, Naples, surely you've heard of Naples, the famous Italian Port?"*

Tired Business Man: *"No, how much is it a bottle?"*

THE REMINISCENT TODDY

(Senator Tydings *of Maryland has represented his state in a truly masterful manner. Although one of the younger members of the Senate he has made his presence felt on all matters of importance. That he has ever been able to keep an even balance in times of turbulence probably is due to a large extent to a well defined sense of humor appropriately applied.*)

This potation, to be thoroughly enjoyed, should be prepared in the following manner:

Supply each guest with a glass containing about one-half

inch of water and one-quarter teaspoonful of sugar, and a spoon.

All should sit comfortably and stir the sugar until it is thoroughly dissolved. The host should tell the following story in a low voice while the sugar is being stirred:

"Have you gentlemen ever participated at a Kentucky breakfast?"

The answer is likely to be in the negative. Then some guest will probably ask:

"What is a Kentucky breakfast?"

At this point the sugar is completely dissolved. The host passes around a bottle of Bourbon and each person pours into his glass, containing the dissolved sugar, such amount as suits his inclination. This is stirred for a while, during which time the host replies:

"A Kentucky breakfast is a big beefsteak, a quart of Bourbon and a houn' dawg."

One of the guests will then ask:

"What is the dog for?"

The host then replies:

"He eats the beefsteak."

Ice water is then passed around in a silver pitcher to dilute the drink to meet the requirements of the discriminating taste of each. A part of the Kentucky breakfast is then consumed.

(In order to extract the nth power of enjoyment from this receipt, when stirring the sugar and water, each should sit on the very edge of his chair or sofa, rest his arms on his knees with a slightly forward posture. Unless this is done the drink will taste just a little less good.)—*Senator Millard Tydings, Harford County*.

MONTPELIER, PRINCE GEORGE'S COUNTY

("MONTPELIER" *was built on a part of the original grant of ten thousand acres to Richard Snowden in 1719. Thomas Snowden started the manor that was destined to become on several occasions the stopping place of that intimate friend of the family, George Washington. It is one of the most satisfying of all Maryland Manors and its boxwood gardens certainly cannot be surpassed for beauty throughout the State.*

The charming old home is now fortunately owned by the Hon. Breckinridge Long, who cherishes and protects its traditions and beauty.)

APPLE TODDY

Twelve apples, a little tart, red streaks if possible, or wine sap, roasted or baked and mashed to one gallon water; sweetened to the taste, say one and one-half pounds sugar, four tumblerfuls of brandy, one of rum, one of peach brandy, mix thoroughly and add of above liquids if necessary.—*Miss Caroline Snowden Fairfax, great-great-granddaughter of Thomas Snowden, Princ ·George's County*

SYLLABUB

Season rich milk with sugar and wine, but not enough to curdle it. Fill the glasses nearly full and crown them with whipped cream seasoned.—*Mrs. George H. Birnie, Carroll County.*

ROMAN PUNCH

6 oranges, 4 lemons, 1 quart whiskey or 1 bottle champagne, 8 egg whites, 2 pounds sugar, 1 gallon water. Grate the rinds and add to the juice, one gallon water, one quart whiskey and 8 whites of eggs beaten to a froth. Freeze.—*Mrs. Robert Goldsborough Henry, Myrtle Grove, Talbot County.*

APPLE TODDY

One dozen apples well roasted, one gallon of hot water, one quart of brandy, one pint peach brandy, one powdered nutmeg, a few allspice and cloves. Cover up in a pitcher and let it remain three or four days.

In the above receipt, peel the roasted apples and pour the brandy over the pulp, letting it stand a little while to extract the flavor.—*Dr. Walter Forman Wickes, Wickcliffe, Greenspring Valley, Baltimore County.*

CANDIES

WALNUT TAFFY

2 cups of molasses, piece of butter size of egg, 1 good size cup of picked out black walnuts. Boil hard. Drop a little in cup of cold water, when brittle stir in walnuts, then pour out in a sheet. When perfectly cold cut or break up in pieces.—*Miss Mary W. Crisfield, Somerset County.*

FLUFFY RUFFLE CANDY

Two cups granulated sugar, one-quarter cup water, one-half cup corn syrup, boil, until nearly hard when tested in water, and pour very slowly into the beaten whites of two eggs, beat until stiff but not too stiff to pour. Add flavoring and one cup of nuts to be added before it gets too stiff.—*Mrs. W. B. Deen, Caroline County.*

TAFFY CARAMELS

Put one-quarter lb. chocolate, four ounces butter, one pound brown sugar, one-half cup molasses, one-half cup cream and vanilla into saucepan. Cook slowly and until mixture hardens when dropped in cold water.—*Miss Mary McDaniel, Talbot County.*

SUGAR CARAMEL

Two cups sugar, three ounces of Baker's chocolate, one large tablespoonful of butter, ¾ cup cream or rich milk. Cook until it hardens in cold water and stir in ¼ cup of powdered sugar. Add one tablespoon of vanilla.—*Dr. Walter Forman Wickes, Wickcliffe, Greenspring Valley, Baltimore County.*

"Have you time to sew this button on, Dearest?"
"Sorry but I haven't. I'm following out this receipt, and it says not to stir for ten minutes."

WALNUT CANDY

One-half pound of English walnuts, one pound of confectioners' sugar, one tablespoonful of vanilla, one tablespoonful of water, one white of an egg. Mix the egg and sugar together, then add the vanilla and water. Roll in little balls and put the walnuts on each side.—*Dr. Walter Forman Wickes, Wickcliffe, Greenspring Valley, Baltimore County.*

COCONUT CANDY

One coconut grated, one and one-half pounds sugar. Pour the milk of the coconut over the sugar. Heat slowly. Boil eight minutes. Add coconut and boil ten minutes. Pour on to a buttered platter. Let stand twenty-four hours. Cut in squares and turn over. Let dry on the outside. Put away in boxes.—*Mrs. George H. Birnie, Carroll County.*

CHOCOLATE FUDGE

Melt quarter pound chocolate in double boiler, then add:—1 pound XXXX sugar, 10 marshmallows, ½ cup milk, 1 tablespoonful butter, 1 teaspoonful vinegar, a pinch of salt. Boil slowly until it begins to thicken, then take from fire and beat until light. Pour in buttered pan and cut in squares when hardened. Nuts may be added if desired.—*Mrs. Ida Kenney, Baltimore.*

MARSHMALLOWS

One envelope of Knox's sparkling gelatine, one and one-quarter cups water, two cups fine granulated sugar and a few grains of salt, one teaspoonful of vanilla. Soak gelatine in one-half the water five minutes, put remaining water and sugar in saucepan and bring to boiling point, and boil until syrup will spin a thread when dropped from tip of spoon, add soaked gelatine and let stand until practically cool, then add salt and flavoring, beat until mixture becomes white and thick. Pour into pan thickly dusted with powdered sugar, place until chilled. Turn on board, cut in blocks.—*Mrs. W. B. Deen, Caroline County.*

"The most indispensable quality of a good cook is promptness. It should also be that of the guests."—BRILLAT-SAVARIN.

CREAM MINTS

Four cups white sugar, one-quarter of a quarter pound cake of butter, eight cups of water. Flavor with a few drops of oil of peppermint. Cook until it cracks against the glass when spoon is put into cold water. Pour on to a marble slab and pull until hard. This turns creamy after a few hours.—*Mrs. George H. Birnie, Carroll County.*

APPENDICES

APPENDIX A

ELKRIDGE HOUNDS

No reference to Maryland life could be complete without reference to the fox hunt clubs which have been so completely a part of Maryland since the first hounds were imported from England by the Colonists.

The Elkridge Hounds at Long Quarter Farm in the Dulaney Valley is the second oldest in the United States and was established in 1872. One looks far for as inspiring a sight as the Elkridge Hounds in full pursuit across Baltimore and Harford Counties. Below is a menu of a typical hunt luncheon of the Elkridge Hounds, served on a long table in the middle of the room, as served on Thanksgiving or New Years:

HUNT LUNCHEON OF THE ELKRIDGE HOUNDS AS OF THANKS-GIVING OR NEW YEARS

Hot Bouillon
Roast Suckling Pig—stuffed with potatoes with a red apple in his mouth
Old Maryland Ham

Roast Turkey
      Spoon Bread from water ground white corn meal from old mill in
their hunting country
         Cranberries
         Hominy
         Mushrooms
         Scrambled Eggs
         Celery Salad
         Mince Pie
         Ice Cream
         Hot Rolls
         Coffee
         Nuts
         Olives

APPENDIX B

BILL OF FARE OF THE GRAND BANQUET OF THE RAILWAYS CELEBRATIONS
OF 1857 AT THE MARYLAND INSTITUTE

Soups

Green Turtle   Soup à la Julienne

Fish

Boiled Salmon, Lobster Sauce
Boiled Sheepshead, White Sauce
Striped Bass, Baked, Genoise Sauce
Chesapeake Bay Mackerel, à la Maître d'Hôtel

Relishes

Worcestershire Sauce   French Mustard   Assorted Pickles
Apple Sauce   Currant Jelly   Cucumbers
Olives   Anchovy

Boiled

Ham   Lamb   Spring Chicken

Entrees

Filets de Boeuf, Madeira Wine Sauce
Petites Patés, à la Reine
Sweet Bread, Larded Gardinere Sauce
Fillets of Veal, Perageaux Sauce
Vol au Vent, à la Financier
Young Chickens, Maryland Style

Mountain Oysters, Sauce Royale
Beuder à la Richelieu, Tomato Sauce
Lamb Chops, Soubaise Sauce
Timbale de Macaroni, Milanaise
Galantine de Poulets

Maryland Course

Roast Saddle of Mountain Mutton, Currant Jelly Sauce

Soft Crabs Fried, Butter and Parsley
    Sauce
Soft Crabs, Broiled
Hard Crabs, Deviled

Summer Ducks, with Olives
Green Goose, Apple Sauce
Roast Ham, Champagne Sauce

Vegetables

Stewed Tomatoes
Green Corn
Boiled Beets

Baked Tomatoes
String Beans
Cymlings

Green Peas
Boiled Potatoes

Cold and Ornamental Dishes

Ham on a Pedestal, decorated with Jelly
Boned Turkey, on a Socle, French Style

Poulets Trufflé, à la Belle Vue
Boeuf Salé, en Presse
Lobster Salad, Mayonnaise
Paté of Liver Jelly
Aspic d'Huitres

Salade de Poulets Historée
Buffalo Tongues, Garnished with Jelly
Sliced Tomatoes, à la Harden
Crab Salad, Baltimore Fashion

Ornamented Pieces and Dessert

Emblem of Commerce
Ancient Cornucopia
Corbeille Renaissance
Corbeille Antique
Pyramides la Amors
Pyramide la Dolphin
Nougat Casket
Pyramides Dessert

Madeira Wine
Punch Cakes
Vanilla Ice Cream
Almond Ice Cream
Strawberry Ice Cream
Orange Ice Cream
Raspberry Ice Cream
Pine Apple Ice Cream

313

Bisquit Glacée, au Cream Caisse	Caramel Ice Cream
Charlotte Russe	Plumbier
Maraschino	Bisquit Glacée au Chorolade
Charlotte Russe (Lemon)	Fancy Cakes
Jelly Rum Maraschino	

Fruits and Flowers

Water Melons   Apples   Oranges   Pine Apples   Pears
Bananas   Apricots   Raspberries
Pyramids, Bouquets and Baskets of Flowers, in every variety

APPENDIX C

ACCOUNT FOR AN ENTERTAIN.

ON THE NEWS OF PEACE

IN APRIL LAST

GEORGE MANN

£280. 2. 4

24TH DEC. 1783

ENT.

STATE DEBT

1783
April 24th

The State of Maryland.........Dr

To Geo Mann.........

	£		
To 49 Gallons Clarret @ 20/...........................	49	0	0
To 35 Gallons port Wine @ 20/........................	35		
To 32 Gallons Madaira Wine @ 22/6....................	36		
To 6 Gallons Spirits @ 15/............................	4	10	
To 15 lb. Loaf Sugar @ 2/.............................	1	10	
To 176 lb. Bacon @ 10d...............................	7	6	8
To 284 lb. Salt Beef @ 7d.............................	8	5	8
To 52 lb. Shoat @ 6d.................................	1	6	
To 126 lb. Mutton @ 8d...............................	4	4	
To 272 lb. Veal @ 8d..................................	9	1	4
To 183 lb. Beef Roasted @ 7d.........................	5	13	5
To 12 fowles @ 2/24/, 7 Lambs @ 20/140/..............	8	4	

Item	£	s	d
To Dressing and finding the above for dinner.............	37	10	
For the Ball....			
To 8 Gallons Wine @ 22/6...........................	9		
To 4 Gallon Spirits @ 15/...........................	3		
To 2 hams wt. 23 lb. @ 10d 19/2 ⎫			
To 2 Rounds Beef wt. 42 lb. @ 7d 24/6................ ⎬ 2	3	8	
To 6 Tongues 30/, 10 fowles 20/, a Turkey 5/........... ⎭ 2	15		
To Tarts, Custards and Cheese Cakes.....................	2	10	
To finding and Dressing the above for Sup..............	6		
To 592 Loaves Bread @ 6d..........................	14	16	
To Cards 24/, Candles 35/...........................	2	19	
To 35 Knives and 29 forks lost.......................	2	16	
To 28 Queens Ware Plates Lost 46/8, 43 wine glasses 71/8	5	18	4
To one Queens Ware Dish............................		17	6
To Waiters and Attendance at the Ball..................	3	5	
To Musick 155/, 61 Bottles 25/5.....................	9	0	5
	£272	12	0
Cr. By one Box of Candles wt. 60 lb. @ 2/.............	6	0	0
Ballance Due G. M.......	£266	12	0
Brought over Carried over			
To 3 Loaves Sugar which Mr. Crisall had of Mr. Randall Wt. 27 lb. 14 oz. @ 2/......	2	14	10
	£269	6	10
Interest thereon to the 24th December 1783. 8 Months......	10	15	6
Due on the above account provided for an Entertainment for celebrating the News of peace............. ⎬	£280	2	4

Examined and passed

C. Richmond Aud. Gen.

Rec. an Order on the U. S. Treasurer for the above amt.

Geo Mann

APPENDIX D

EXPENSE OF ENTERTAINT.

TO GENL. WASHINGTON

GEO MANN

66. 11. 0

4TH DEC. 1784

ENTD.

S. DEBT

The State of Maryland..............Dr
To Geo Mann........

To 63 1/3 lb. Beef @ 8...................................	2	2	4
To 23¾ lb. Baccon @ 1/6.............................	1	15	6
To 5 Tongues @ 4/6...................................	1	2	6
To 4 Turkeys @ 5/...................................	1	0	0
To 12 fowles @ 2/...................................	1	4	0
	£7	4	4
To finding and Dressing the above.....................	7	4	4
To Tarts, Custards and Cke...........................	6	14	
To 17 lb. Cake @ 2/...................................	1	14	
To Bread 20/, Candles 23/4, Cards 15/................	2	18	4
To Wood and Drawing 18/, sugar 20/, Musick 125/......	8	3	
To 42 Bottles Madeira @ 7/6.........................	15	15	
To 21 Bottles port Wine @ 5/.........................	5	5	
To 4 Gallons Spirits @ 11/3...........................	2	5	
To 150 Lemons.......................................	4	2	6
To Porter 15/, Sallard pickles 10/.....................	1	5	
To a Chair Broak 10/, Glasses Broak 3/................		13	
To Waiters 37/6, Cleaning the room @ attendance at the Door 15/	2	12	6
To attendance in the Bar.............................		15	
	£66	11	

Auditors Office 4th December 1784
The above account proved examined and passed for Sixty Six Pounds Eleven
Shillings

C. Richmond
Aud. Gen.

Rec'd the Contents per order on the Treasurer W. Shore
Geo. Mann

APPENDIX E

ACCOUNT FOR AN

ENTERTAINMENT TO HIS

EXCELLY GEN. WASHINGTON

THE 22D DECM. 1783

PD. G. MANN £71. 6. 6

ENT.

STATE DEBT

1783
Decem. 22

The State of Maryland................Dr
To Geo Mann.........

To a Supper at the State House.......................	£17	12	6
To 98 Bottles Wine..................................	36	15	
To 2½ gallon Spirits.................................	1	17	6
To 9 lb. Loaf Sugar 10/, Service 25/....................	2	3	
To Musick	5	17	6
To Waiters 45/, attendance in the Bar 35/..............	4		
To 12 packs of Cards 22/6...........................	1	2	6
To 8 lb. Candles.....................................		16	
To Cleaning the Rooms	1	2	6
	71	6	6

Due on Account of an Entertainment, ⎫
given by the Legislature to his   ⎬
Excellency Gen. Washington   ⎭
Examined and passed 24th Dec. 1783
C. Richmond Aud. Genl.
RECEIVED an Order on the U. S. Treasurer for the above amt.
Geo. Mann

INDEX

SOUP

OYSTERS

TERRAPIN

SEA FOOD

GAME

FOWL

FOWL—*Continued*

Chicken à la Tudor Hall, 88
Chicken à la Marengo, 88
Chicken Livers with Pilaff Indienne, 90
Spanish Chicken, 90
Chicken with Noodles, 90
Panned Chicken, 92
Chicken Maryland, 93
Stewed Chicken, 94
Boned Squab Chicken with Dressing, 94
Giblet Hash with Poached Egg, 94

Roast Goose, 96
Roasted Guinea Hen, 96
Deviled Turkey Legs, 96
Boneless Turkey, 96
Turkey Stuffing, 98
Stuffed Roast Squab, 98
Panned Chickens, 99
Curry, 100
Braised Duckling Bigarrade, 100
Roast Turkey, 101

EGGS

Poached Eggs with Tomatoes and Mush-
rooms, 105
Eggs à la Crême, 105
Egg Croquettes, 106
Eggs in Aspic, 107
Omelette Soufflé, 108
Scrambled Eggs, 108

Maryland Omelet, 108
Spanish Omelette, 109
Marsh Hen Eggs, 110
Eggs, Jockey Club, 110
Shirred Eggs, 110
Eggs with Tomato and Rice, 111

MEATS

Roast Beef and Gravy, 115
Beef Tongue, 115
Roast Beef, 117
Mince of Lamb, 117
Roulade of Beef with Mushrooms, 118
Beef Kidney Stew, 118
Corning Beef, 118
To Cook a Beefsteak, 119
Brunswick Stew, 120
Baked Calf's Head, 120
Pan Rarebit, 121
Lamb Chop Brasseur, 121
Fried Liver, 121
Calf's Head—Whole, 122
Hog's Head Cheese, 123
Pig's Feet, Chafing Dish, 123
Platter Dinner, 124
Meat Soufflé, 125
Creamed Calves' Brains, 125

Pork Chops, 125
Sweetbreads, 126
Colonial Maryland Sausage, 126
To Stew Mutton Chops, 127
Sausage Meat, 127
Mock Terrapin in Chafing Dish, 128
Country Sausage, 128
Sausage, 128
Sausage, 129
Scrapple, 130
Woodmont Club Famous Sausage, 130
Ragout Sweetbreads—Chamillon, 131
Swiss Steak, 131
Jellied Tongue, 132
Veal Croquettes, 132
Veal Pate Jelly, 132
Pressed Veal or Chicken with Egg, 133
Yorkshire Pudding, 134

THE COOKING AND STUFFING OF HAMS AND THE CURING OF MEATS AFTER THE FASHION OF OLD MARYLAND MANORS

VEGETABLES

SALADS AND SALAD DRESSINGS

SAUCES

BREADS

CAKES AND PASTRIES

CAKES AND PASTRIES—*Continued*

JELLIES, PRESERVES AND PICKLES

PUDDINGS

DESSERTS

BEVERAGES

CANDIES